The Complete
FISHERMAN

The Complete
FISHERMAN

A GUIDE TO FISHING THROUGH THE YEAR

Graham Marsden · Brian Furzer · John Darling

WARD LOCK LIMITED · LONDON

Designed by Bob Swan
Text filmset in 10 point Sabon
By Tradespools Ltd, Frome, Somerset

Printed and bound in Singapore by
Toppan Printing Co.

British Library Cataloguing in Publication Data

Marsden, Graham
 The complete fisherman.
 1. Fishing—Great Britain
 I. Title   II. Furzer, Brian   III. Darling, John
 799.1'2'0941   SH605
 ISBN 1-85079-188-0

Acknowledgments

The publishers would like to thank the following
for supplying photographs for the book.

Colour: John Carding front endpaper; Geoff
Chesterman 70; Arthur Clarke title page; Nick
Cranfield 55; John Darling 50, 58, 83, 87, 90, 91,
94–5, 98, 102, 103, 106, 107, 110–11, 115, 119,
122, back endpaper; Steve Harper 35; Trevor
Housby 78; Graham Marsden 15, 22, 23, 27, 38,
42, 43; Neil Nevison 50; Barrie Roberts 7, 30, 33;
John Tarlton 75; John Watson 19, 26.

Black and white: Dave Collyer 67; Nick Cranfield
49 top and bottom, 70; John Darling 81, 84, 88,
89, 99, 104, 108, 109, 113, 117, 120, 125, 127,
128, 131; Jens Ploug Hansen 77; Graham Marsden
12, 40; John Tarlton 64, 69, 71, 72.

Line illustrations on pages 133–7 drawn by Tony
Whieldon; those on pages 16, 17, 32, 36, 51, 52,
54 and 138–9 drawn by Bob Mathias.

**Fishing tackle for front jacket photograph kindly
lent by Frames Fishing Tackle, The Broadway,
West Hendon, London NW9.**

Contents

PART I
COARSE FISHING

Coarse fishing on stillwaters

Coarse fishing on rivers

Graham Marsden with a big catch of tench to almost 6 lb (2.7 kg).

Coarse fishing on stillwaters

INTRODUCTION

Included in the stillwater category are ponds, lakes, canals, meres, flashes, reservoirs, gravel and sandpits, and the giant lochs and loughs of Scotland and Ireland.

They are called stillwaters because they have no appreciable flow, although it is a mistake to think that even the common farm pond is completely still. It is a fact that there are subtle currents and eddies on the calmest days in the smallest waters, and there can be extremely powerful currents in very large stillwaters when a strong wind has been blowing for several hours.

Even so, for most of the time when fishing a stillwater you will be fishing what at least appears to be just that, and tackle and tactics are chosen accordingly.

SUMMER: TENCH AND CARP

The summer period, as far as coarse fishing is concerned, will be from the beginning of the season, 16 June, to sometime in September. I say sometime because, obviously, summer does not change to autumn overnight, and it will depend on the weather just when the blend from summer to autumn takes place.

Generally, this will be in the second or third week in September, but in poor summers the change will be apparent much sooner, and in long, hot summers (we have had a few!) the change will only be apparent in the last week of the month, or even in the first week of October. However, as there is no clear-cut dividing line between the seasons, we can only generalize, and generally speaking, summer coarse fishing begins on 16 June and ends around the middle of September, a period of about three months.

In June, July and August water temperatures will be at their highest, and there will be many calm, windless days when waters will appear to be lifeless and stagnant. On such days fish will be disinclined to move and the angler must fish the dawn or dusk period, or even through the night, to enjoy the best sport.

The plant and animal life in stillwaters will also be at its peak, and the angler finds he is fighting a constant battle with this natural food to capture the fish's attention. Many times on particularly rich waters fish become totally preoccupied with a certain food creature when that creature suddenly becomes available in huge numbers.

A strong wind in summer comes, quite literally, like a breath of fresh air. It imparts oxygen to the water and this is what the fish need to liven them up and give them an appetite. A good strong wind also stirs up the natural food and consequently colours the water, which is again in favour of feeding fish.

This, however, applies only to the bigger, mature fish, for the smaller, immature ones are almost always willing to feed in the summer months in all kinds of conditions and at any time of day.

Summing up, the best time to fish the summer months is early morning, late evening, or through the night, unless, that is, we are fishing for small fish which are willing to feed at almost any time. An exception to this is when a strong wind strikes up, which is often responsible for encouraging fish to feed throughout the day, particularly if it is dull and heavily overcast.

Every species of coarse fish that swims can be caught in the summer period, but two species can be singled out as being particularly suitable for the angler's attention at this time of year: the tench and the carp. Tench are particularly a summer fish, and there is no doubt whatsoever that the first two or three weeks of the season is the very best time of all to catch them. Carp can be caught even in the winter, but there is no question that they are essentially a summer fish, in their element when browsing through lily pads on steaming hot days.

Tench

The first two or three weeks of the season is traditionally the time to go tench fishing and, while many

Fishing on a hot summer's day is most enjoyable, but bites can be slow to come.

traditions are based on fancy rather than fact, this is one tradition that deserves to be honoured. There are more tench caught in this relatively short period than during the rest of the season added together. This is not only because more anglers are fishing for them, but also because the tench are far more willing to feed on anglers' baits at this time than any other. Furthermore, the majority of tench are caught in the early morning period: for two to three hours following first light.

Tench are bottom feeders and it is there that you should present your baits. However, before doing this, it is essential to choose the right swim, for like all fish they have favoured areas and are not spread evenly through a water. Plant life is very attractive to tench, particularly lilies, bistort and Canadian pondweed; in fact any weedy area of a fishery is worthy of investigation. You should look for the tiny, tell-tale bubbles that erupt at the surface when tench are grubbing for food in the bottom mud. You may see mud-clouds billowing from the bottom, or even the olive-green or bronze back of a tench as it rolls through the surface.

One way in which you can attract tench to a swim is

On many stillwaters, the margins may be very soft, and even swampy. A solid platform will enable you to fish in safety and comfort.

by raking the bottom. Tie two rake heads together back to back and attach these to a strong rope. Throw the rake into the swim and draw it slowly back towards you several times. This will stir up the bottom mud and expose those tiny creatures that tench love to eat. In addition, tench are very curious fish—the cats of the underwater world—and will soon come to investigate a raked swim. It often pays to scatter groundbait and hookbait samples, such as maggots or worms, over the swim; then rake it to mix them up with the bottom mud. To finish off, scatter a little more groundbait and hookbait samples.

For tench fishing, a rod of 12 ft (3.65 m) in length and about 1¼ lb (550 g) test curve is best. This will be good for float fishing and for legering. A fixed-spool reel, and a line of 3 lb (1.35 kg) for fishing in open water, and 5 lb (2.25 kg) for those heavily weeded, snaggy areas, will be a match for the rod. You need hooks in sizes ranging from 16 to 6, and a selection of lead-substitute split shot.

The float, which need be only a simple piece of peacock quill, should be set as in figure 1, which is a conventional 'laying on' rig. And for legering, an ordinary link-leger is adequate, as in figure 2. The Arlesey bomb can be replaced with a swimfeeder if desired. However, most tench fishing is done at short range, therefore float fishing is the most efficient method.

Although your swim might be raked and baited as described, it is often necessary to keep it 'topped up' with loose feed. This means throwing in a helping of maggots, worms or sweetcorn, which are three of the best baits for tench, at regular intervals while fishing. How often you introduce this loose feed will be governed by how well the tench are feeding on the day.

An important point to remember about tench is that they rarely stick to the same bait throughout a fishing session of more than two or three hours. They can go through a range of baits and then return to the one you began with, so take a good selection with you; the three I have already recommended plus one or two others, such as bread and luncheon meat. Then you can ring the changes when the bites begin to dwindle. The only item of tackle you need to change is the hook, using one to suit the size of bait you have selected.

15

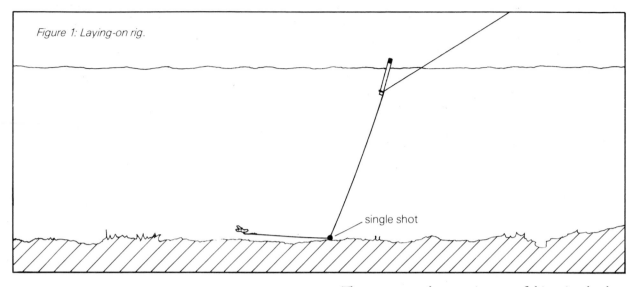

Figure 1: Laying-on rig.

single shot

Carp

King carp come in three forms: the mirror, which has few but large irregularly placed scales; the leather, which has no scales at all; and the common, which is fully scaled. They all belong to the same family and all are fished for in the same way. Carp are mainly bottom feeders, but at times they can also be seen sucking food from the surface. Locating carp in such an instance is easy; you simply watch for the splashes and swirls.

Locating the bottom feeders is not quite as easy, but certainly not difficult, for there are various ways in which they disclose their presence. Mud-clouds and bubbles are two signs, and, of course, surface activity, for they will go down to the bottom to feed even when apparently feeding at the surface. If there are no signs of fish, concentrate on the weedy margins of a lake, the perimeter of islands, the gravel and sand bars in a pit, and any area where there is character on the bottom, such as ledges.

An 11 ft (3.35 m) rod of 1½ lb (700 g) test curve is the standard rod required. This should be married to a fixed-spool reel with a range of lines from 6 lb (2.70 kg) to 12 lb (5.50 kg) breaking strain. Hooks in sizes from 10 to 2, swivels and Arlesey bombs complete the basic tackle requirements. You can, of course, and this applies to legering for any species, buy all kinds of sophisticated auxilliary equipment, such as electric bite alarms, but these are a luxury rather than a necessity.

Stealth and caution are essential when carp fishing, for these fish will patrol in the marginal area when left undisturbed. This close proximity to the fish also means that free-line tackle, that is, with nothing on the line except hook and bait, is a feasible set-up. Otherwise, a light link-leger (figure 2) is usually ideal.

The greatest advances in carp fishing in the last decade or so have involved baits. During this time, two new types of bait have been developed: particle baits and high protein (HP) baits. 'New' does not mean that they have never been used before; no doubt some of them have. It means that carp anglers have developed them, by experiment and persistence, into highly sophisticated and successful weapons with an importance hitherto unheard of in fish baits.

Particle baits are any kind of bait which is relatively small and can be used in quite large quantities. The most well-known particle bait is the maggot, although the maggot is not really regarded as a carp bait. The most popular and widely-used particle baits are sweetcorn, various peas and beans, tares and all kinds of seeds generally obtainable from pigeon and poultry food merchants and Asian food shops. Very small seeds, such as hemp and buckwheat, are known as 'mass' baits, but are used in exactly the same way as particle baits.

The usual, and probably the best, way of using particle baits, is to introduce them to the swim for at least a few days before fishing, and then to feed them on a little-and-often basis during fishing; how little and how often depends on how well the fish are feeding, but a pint of seeds is usually ample for a session of several hours.

On most waters you can use several seeds on a big hook, for example, four grains of sweetcorn on a size 6, but there are a few waters where the fish are exceptionally wary and one or two grains on a size 10 is better. The end tackle should be a link-leger, stopped about 12 in (30.5 cm) from the hook, but if the carp begin to give 'bite-offs', that is, they give a good bite, but upon striking and retrieving the tackle, the line is found to have been bitten through near to the hook,

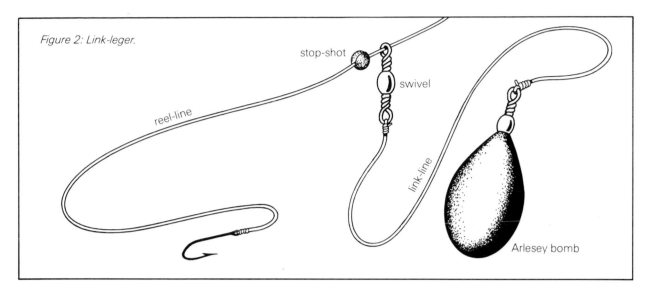

Figure 2: Link-leger.

stop-shot

swivel

reel-line

link-line

Arlesey bomb

then a heavier lead stopped about 2 in (5 cm) from the hook is usually the answer.

HP baits are mixtures of high protein ingredients. The basis of such baits can be meat, fish or even a milk product. One HP bait, which is fairly typical of these mixtures, is: 4 oz (115 g) fish meal, 3 oz (85 g) dried milk, 3 oz (85 g) soya flour, bound together with 3 to 6 eggs. If smaller fish, or any fish other than carp, are proving a nuisance by constantly nibbling at the bait, it can be made into hookbait-sized balls and dipped in boiling water for one to three minutes. This will give the bait a tough skin and render it proof against nuisance fish.

Nevertheless, do not neglect the more conventional baits such as worms and bread, or the pastes made from pet foods, cheese, luncheon meat, and so on, for there are still many waters where these baits will catch plenty of fish. It is only on the more difficult, and

heavily-fished, waters that HP baits are almost essential.

HP baits can be used for prebaiting just as particle baits can be, but obviously in fewer numbers. All you need to do is roll the bait up into hookbait-sized balls and introduce them to the swim for several days before fishing.

The end-tackle can be the same as is used with particle baits, but bite-offs are not usually a problem with paste baits. Bigger hooks, such as sizes 4 and 2, are more common, but the hook point should always be left exposed, otherwise you can miss many bites.

Carp can be caught from the surface, too. Free-line tackle is a good bet when the carp are close to the side, or a long link-leger tackle as in figure 3 when they're too far distant to be reached with almost weightless tackle. The bait can be a crust or anything else that will float.

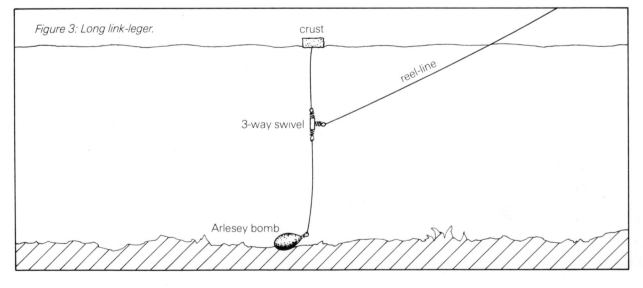

Figure 3: Long link-leger.

crust

reel-line

3-way swivel

Arlesey bomb

Left *This 5 lb (2.2 kg) tench came from a Norfolk lake.*

Above *John Watson with a mirror carp of at least 20 lb (9 kg).*

AUTUMN: BREAM

Autumn is usually the most consistently productive period of the year for stillwater fishing. With the exception of tench, which are without doubt a confirmed summer species, autumn is a marvellous season for catching any coarse fish.

In summer, water temperatures leap upwards during the hot days, and plunge downwards during the relatively cold nights. But in autumn there is less difference between day-time and night-time temperatures, resulting in a more stable water temperature throughout a twenty-four hour period. This encourages the fish to feed at regular intervals, rather than fasting for spells and then gorging themselves occasionally, as they are prone to do in summer.

By the time autumn arrives, around the middle of September, fish are well established on feeding routes and in specific swims. Their wanderlust is curbed to some extent, giving the angler a better chance to track them down, and the almost certain knowledge that once located, they can be found in the same swim on subsequent visits for the remainder of the autumn period.

All coarse fish are in prime condition in autumn, the rigours of spawning are long since over and the recovery complete. This is the time of year when the biggest specimens are likely to be caught; specimens whose weight is not falsely enhanced with pounds of spawn.

Night fishing in autumn is still well worthwhile on stillwaters, though the nights are long and extremely bleak when the fish are hard to come by. Surprisingly, there are many nights when the conditions are warmer and more comfortable than in summer, but the long dark hours take their toll and it pays to take plenty of warm clothing and hot drinks. Although night fishing is still a worthwhile proposition, the steady temperatures and shorter days mean that the chances of catching fish all through the day are greatly improved. Some of my biggest catches and best specimens have been taken around midday in autumn. Sometimes it almost seems as though fish know that winter is just around the corner and they feed more than ever while they still have the inclination.

It is very difficult to single out any one or two species for special attention in autumn for, as already indicated, practically all coarse species are in the peak of condition and wide open to capture during this period. Nevertheless, for stillwater fishing in autumn I choose bream, for all the reasons already mentioned; they are a fine species to wind up my stillwater fishing before winter sets in and my thoughts turn mainly to rivers.

Bream are deep-bodied, almost flat fish with a shoaling instinct second to none. However, their shape makes it difficult for them to fight hard. Nevertheless, the fight you get from fish is relative to the tackle you use to catch them and bream of 3 lb (1.35 kg) or so in weight, which is about average on most bream waters, fight well enough on light tackle.

Apart from very big bream of 8 lb (3.6 kg) and over that are caught, usually in ones and twos, the essence of bream fishing is to catch plenty of them in one sitting. This is possible because bream feed in huge shoals, and the art of catching a big netful is to fish and feed with a sweet rhythm, backed by good judgment as to when and how much loose feed to give them. You can catch plenty of bream only if you are able to keep the shoal in your swim for long enough to do it, and you can only do that by giving them enough, and only just enough, free feed to keep them interested.

Before we look at this feeding business, let us first discuss how to find the bream. After all, location of the shoal is of prime importance, without which all other considerations are worthless.

Bream, on most waters, have a pleasing habit of rolling at the surface both prior to, and during, feeding. They do this along the whole length of a 'beat' (an established feeding route) through an area of a fishery. These beats vary in length and pattern, some are fairly straight for perhaps 100 yd (90 m), others may be semi-circular and cover 400 yd (365 m).

The angler who is trying to locate bream, especially the average-sized bream of around 3 lb (1.35 kg), need rarely do more than visit the proposed water and watch for this rolling performance, which is most likely to be seen in the early morning and late evening, but can occur whenever the bream choose to feed.

Make a careful note of every spot where the bream are seen to roll, and from this deduce the full extent of the feeding route. What you must realize is that, although the bream can be persuaded to feed with the use of free feed, at any point along the route there are specific spots where they feed naturally, and if these areas are baited and fished they are far more productive than anywhere else. Such areas are normally at the point where the route veers off at a tangent, or at the terminal point of a route.

For some reason, we can only speculate about why mature bream are almost always found at least 25 yd (20 m) from the margins, although this is not so with small, immature bream, known as skimmers. It is, therefore, common practice on most waters to leger for the sizeable bream with tackle suitable for long-range fishing. Fishing for skimmers in the margins and up to about 10 yd (9 m) out can be accomplished with conventional float or leger tackle.

The rod for distance legering should be 11 ft (3.35 m) long with a medium-fast taper and a test curve of around 1¼ lb (550 g). It should have a threaded tip-ring to accommodate a swingtip or quivertip.

The best reel is, of course, a fixed-spool type which should be filled to the brim with 3 lb (1.35 kg) line. It is important that the spool should be completely filled so that the long casting necessary – often as much as 70 yd (65 m) can be achieved. If the line lies too low in the spool it has too far to climb with a resulting loss of distance through friction.

The most efficient tackle for long-range legering for bream is a fixed paternoster. This consists of a tiny swivel with the reel line tied to the top eye. Tied to the bottom eye is a 9 in (22.85 cm) length of the reel line with an Arlesey bomb tied at the end. Also tied to the bottom eye of the swivel is the hook length which is usually 1 yd (1 m) long and 2½ lb (1.15 kg) breaking strain, but this can be reduced in strength to 2 lb (0.90 kg) breaking strain if thought necessary.

The hook size depends on the size of bait being used, with an 18s, 16s and 14s for one or more maggots or casters, and a 14s or 12s for small redworms and small pieces of bread flake. The hook should be a forged, spade-end type.

The weight of the Arlesey bomb in use will depend on the distance you need to cast and the strength, if any, of cross-winds. The smallest you need will be ¼ oz (7 g) and the largest 1 oz (30 g).

There is no doubt that a swingtip hinders both distance and accuracy when casting, but apart from that it is a very efficient bite indicator. From the moment the tackle hits the surface it is ready to indicate bites, for the tip is at full stretch as the bait sinks, and then hangs slack as soon as the bomb hits bottom. After a few casts you learn how long it takes for the tackle to sink, and if the tip remains straight for a second longer than it should you know the bait has been taken 'on the drop'. This is a common occurrence when fishing amongst a big shoal of feeding bream, and the paternoster, with its long hook length, is designed to take advantage of this 'on the drop' technique.

The swingtip is the ideal indicator when fishing for a big catch of shoal bream, but when fishing for just one or two big bream a better indicator is an electric bite alarm used in conjunction with a clip-on bobbin. Such an indicator allows you to relax and scan the water for signs of fish with the sure knowledge that the audible alarm will alert you at the first sign of a bite.

The most productive bream baits are maggots, casters and small redworms, but an essential ingredient when bream fishing at long range is groundbait,

for there is no way you can reach the swim with loose feed. The groundbait is used solely as a carrying agent for the loose feed. Another essential item then, is a catapult, which should have a moulded rubber or leather cup so as not to compress and crack open the ball of bait when the elastic is stretched back.

The groundbait should be an even mixture of finely ground pure white and brown breadcrumbs. A shallow bowl is the best type of receptacle in which to mix the bait, for this will ensure you mix it thoroughly and get plenty of air in it to make it soft and fluffy. Water should be poured into the bowl first and the groundbait added a little at a time. The loose feed, preferably small feeder maggots (squats) or casters, should be added at this stage. Squats and casters are dormant baits and will not cause the groundbait ball to split in flight. It should then be left to stand for a few minutes while it soaks. You should be able to squeeze the finished groundbait into a ball with one hand and fire the ball to the swim without it breaking in flight, but it should be of a consistency to break up and spread as soon as it hits the surface. This is important, for if the groundbait lies in lumps on the bottom it can be consumed by the bream and will overfeed them in no time. Groundbait is only an attractor and a carrying agent for the loose feed.

Mixing groundbait is your first job when you arrive at the water. This will give it several minutes 'soaking' time while you tackle up, and it should be a perfect consistency when you begin to fire it in.

About a dozen tangerine-sized balls should be fired into the swim to begin with, in a compact circle of no more than about 3 yd (2.75 m) to 4 yd (3.65 m) in diameter. The remainder of the groundbait should be fired in as and when the bream show signs of going off feed and vacating the swim.

This is the most difficult aspect of bream fishing to get right. Too much groundbait and loose feed will overfeed them. Too little and they lose interest and move out of the swim. When the bream are mad on feed it is not a problem. Indeed, there are times when the sound of a ball of groundbait breaking the surface is enough to spur them into a feeding frenzy, as they associate the sound with food and it triggers them off.

Such occasions are rarities, however, compared with the times when they have to be subtly coaxed into a prolonged feeding spell. Then, there is a danger of scaring them off when the groundbait balls hit the surface, which is a good reason for using only small, soft balls of bait that break the surface with the minimum of disturbance.

The actual moment when groundbait should be catapulted into the swim is the most difficult thing to judge. There are some schools who say that you should

Left *Graham Marsden lands a bream.*

Right *Graham Marsden with a 9 lb (4.5 kg) bream that he took from an Irish lough.*

wait until the bream show signs of going off feed and then introduce bait to bring them back on. There are others who reckon the bait should be fired in while the bream are still well on feed as there is less chance of disturbing them while they are still very much pre-occupied with feeding.

I must admit that at one time I went along with the first school of thought, but in recent years I have practised the latter method and find it much better. Whichever method you adopt, it is better to feed little and often than to feed large quantities only rarely. By feeding little and often you ensure that there is always some bait in the swim, but with the other method there is always a danger of the larder becoming bare before you realize it.

If the water is heavily fished, specially if there are regular fishing matches, I would suggest that you begin with a couple of maggots on a size 16 hook and go down to an 18 if the bites are too shy to hit. If, on the other hand, the water is not too heavily fished, it would be better to begin with three of four maggots on a size 14 hook and go down from there if necessary. The alternative is to use an even bigger hook with worm or bread. Very often, too, a cocktail bait of worm and maggot, or maggot and bread, can pay off.

Following the cast, the bale-arm of the reel should be closed and the swing-tip watched carefully as the tackle sinks. As soon as the bomb hits bottom the swing-tip falls slack. Any slack line should then be taken up immediately and the swing-tip again ob-

COARSE FISHING ON STILLWATERS

served very carefully, for although the weight has come to rest the bait is still falling slowly. This is the crucial moment when most bites occur, for the bait is often intercepted as it slowly sinks during those few seconds.

From that moment until you make your next cast you should watch the 'tip for any signs of it lifting or falling back, occasionally inching the bait through the swim. This movement of the bait can spur a bream into grabbing it whereas it may ignore a stationary bait that lies amongst a bed of loose feed that is also stationary. The movement makes the bait that much more noticeable and attracts the bream's attention.

The bait should never be left in the water for long periods to fish for itself. When bream fishing, you have to work at it to make the biggest catches.

There will of course be long periods when there is no action, particularly when you first arrive at the water and the bream are not yet present in the swim. There is then a great temptation to introduce more bait into the swim in the hope that this will spur the bream into feeding. It rarely does. In fact, it can have the opposite effect and frighten off any bream that may have been on the point of tasting a few morsels. Even if it does not frighten off the bream, it may overfeed them very quickly with the result that you catch only one or two fish, rather than a big catch if only you had been patient and fed the swim carefully as and when the bream required it.

With bream, specially on stillwaters in autumn, when the feeding routes are well established, you have to remember that they could be anywhere on this route at the time you begin fishing. If you have ensured that you are fishing over some point on this route, the bream will, almost certainly, enter your swim at some time during your fishing period. If, that is, you are going to be there for several hours. The only aspect in doubt is whether the bream will be hungry enough to feed.

Playing bream on light tackle is a matter of striking without breaking off, and then getting over that initial thump as the bream turns and tries to swim off. The strike should be a controlled sweeping back of the rod until the fish is felt, and then a gentle easing off to allow the fish to bounce on the rod tip. An uncontrolled strike, when your reactions are not tuned to easing off at the right moment, will only lead to a broken line.

Once the initial thumping has passed, it is a relatively simple matter of easing the bream towards the waiting landing net, but being constantly alert to 'kiting', which, with the bream being a deep-bodied fish, is its inclination when too much side-strain is applied. It is best to keep the rod high and to guide the bream gently rather than trying to bully it. It is a good idea to keep the rod high and in one position, rather than swinging it from one side to the other, because of the danger of working the hook loose. The hook can easily fall out if a small one, such as an 18, is in use.

When you have landed a bream, and it is carefully unhooked and placed in a large keepnet, cast a new bait back into the swim as quickly as possible. Bream can move into and out of a swim almost as fast as switching on an electric light, and you have to take full advantage of them while they are there.

WINTER: PIKE

One point to remember always about fish is that they are cold-blooded creatures whose body temperature fluctuates with that of the water. When the body temperature of a fish drops below a certain level—and this varies with each species—it becomes sluggish in its movements; it uses little energy and as a consequence requires little food to replace the lost energy.

In winter, therefore, the angler must remember that fish, as a general rule, feed less often, and eat less when they do feed, than in the warm months. As a counterbalance to this, however, is the fact that the plant and animal life in the water is also lying dead or almost dormant, so the fish, when they do feed, are far more inclined to accept our baits than when there is an abundance of natural food from which to choose.

It is also apparent that fish location is even more important than it is in the warmer months. In summer, and to some extent in autumn, fish move freely through most areas of a fishery, covering considerable distances in relatively short periods. They have favoured areas of course, so it is always important to choose a swim wisely, but with most species, there is a wide margin for error.

In winter this margin for error narrows considerably. Imprecise swim location, even by a few yards (metres), can be punished with a complete blank. In the cold months, when fish are not inclined to wander far, it pays to spend a little more time ensuring you have chosen the right pitch.

Again, though, there is a counterbalance. The extra difficulty of precise swim and fish location is somewhat compensated for by the fact that once located, you can find the fish in the same swim time after time throughout the winter.

The times when fish feed in winter often remain the same, dawn and dusk being most popular. However, for some species, such as carp, bream and perch, winter usually entails a shift in feeding times from the nocturnal and near-nocturnal hours to the midday period, when the sun is at its peak. Fortunately, with the short days of winter, you can, if you wish, fish right through from dawn to dusk and still fish no more than about nine hours.

There is no question that the best species to fish for on a stillwater in winter is the pike. As tench are the traditional summer species, pike are the traditional winter species. They are at their best in winter, sleek and plump, fit and full of fight. They respond to a variety of methods; float-fishing, legering and the various spinning techniques. And spinning can be very welcome on a cold winter's day when the exercise gets the blood flowing again.

Another good winter species is perch, particularly on deep lakes and reservoirs where they take up residence in the deepest holes. They can be relied upon to provide sport in all sorts of foul conditions (apart from an iced-over surface) for the temperature in those deep holes remains at a constant 39.2°F.

Roach, too, are a good winter species, refusing to feed only in the most severe conditions; that is, flat calm and on the point of freezing over. Even in winter, the best time to catch them is from an hour before dark to an hour after.

Pike

Pike are a predatory, fish-eating species, except when circumstances such as lack of prey-fish have forced them to eat other types of food in order to survive. You have only to look at pike; the eyes set on top of the head instead of on the side of the head as in other coarse fish; the long, flat snout; the jaws with row after row of sharp teeth; the camouflaged body, long and slim, with the dorsal fin set well back to assist the tail in sudden bursts of speed. Make no mistake, the pike is a natural killing machine, perfectly designed for speed and efficient movement.

Pike spawn much earlier than most other coarse fish, usually between the end of February and end of March. This is one reason why the winter period, particularly after Christmas, is such a good time to fish for them, for they have to feed to produce the spawn. In addition, a week or two before spawning they congregate on the shallows and the angler who is lucky enough to find them can make a truly memorable catch.

Locating pike is not too difficult. When locating any species the age-old advice is to think like a fish, so if you have trouble thinking like a pike all you have to do is think like a prey-fish, as the pike will not be far away. I am not being flippant; try to think where the prey-fish—the smaller bream, roach, perch or whatever—will be. The pike are never far from a larder.

On the densely populated waters, where vast shoals of small fish can be found in almost every area of the fishery, there is no point in locating prey-fish in order to locate the pike. They will then be in select areas that offer the best ambushing spots. These will be in the vicinity of sunken trees, dense weed-beds and, most popular of all, pike lairs. These occur where the lake bed sharply shelves, and the pike can lie at the base of the shelf ready to pounce on a shoal of victims as they appear, unsuspecting, over the top.

You need a heavy rod for pike, even small pike, to provide the power to impregnate their bony jaws with a set of treble hooks. This means that a rod of at least 2 lb (0.90 kg) test curve is necessary, but one of 2½ lb (1.15 kg) is even better. When choosing a pike rod, you must remember that quite heavy baits, up to 6 oz (180 g) or so, have to be cast. This is not, however, necessarily true of a spinning rod, but this aspect of pike fishing will be dealt with later in the chapter.

Both fixed-spool reels and multiplying reels are well suited to pike fishing. Both have their good and bad points, and you should be guided by personal preference. The fixed-spool reel's main advantage is that it is so well known among coarse fishermen, there are few, even among novice anglers, who do not know how to use one. It is easy to cast long distances with one, and it is almost foolproof as far as tangles are concerned.

Not so the multiplying reel. Over-runs, even with the so-called anti-over-run devices, are still easy to attain in novice hands. Over-runs are caused when the spool continues to revolve after the end-tackle has stopped. Even so, once the technique of casting with a multiplier has been mastered, it is much easier to cast a heavy lead or bait over a long distance. A big fish is easier to control with a multiplier, and it is more suitable for use with heavy lines of 12 lb (5.50 kg) test or more.

I use both types of reel. The fixed-spool when using lines up to 12 lb (5.50 kg) and baits up to about 4 oz (115 g), and a multiplier for baits over 4 oz (115 g) and lines more than 12 lb (5.50 kg) test.

I have used line as low as 6 lb (2.70 kg) breaking strain for pike fishing, but only for the occasional short, 'fun' session for small jack pike. I have also used line as heavy as 18 lb (8 kg) test, but only when fishing big lochs for big pike that hang around rocky territory. For general pike fishing you need a line of no less than 10 lb (4.50 kg) test and no more than 12 lb (5.50 kg) test.

A wire trace is essential, as the many rows of cutting teeth that fill a pike's mouth soon make short work of an ordinary nylon line. The strength of the wire trace should not be less, and is usually a little more, than the strength of the reel-line. It should be attached to the reel-line with a swivel.

Treble hooks from a size 10 to a size 2, while not essential to pike fishing are, nevertheless, preferable to single hooks. One point of the treble can be used to secure the bait, leaving two to hook the pike.

At one time the most commonly used pike floats were those known as 'Fishing Gazette' bungs. However, cigar-shaped floats are much better and are widely available in tackle shops. Otherwise, it is a simple matter to make your own from balsa wood. You can buy or make them in sizes ranging from about 3 in (7.5 cm) to about 6 in (15 cm), to suit various sizes of bait.

Baits for pike are either live or dead fish, but it is becoming increasingly unacceptable to use live-baits due to the increasing attention the sport is receiving from the anti-angling lobbies. In addition, anglers are becoming more conservation-minded and therefore more reluctant to use other coarse fish as live-baits. The alternative is to use a sea species from the fish-monger's slab, the most popular of which are sprats, herrings and mackerel.

Dead-baiting for pike takes two basic forms: the bait suspended off the bottom with float tackle, or legered on the bottom with a conventional leger rig, or laid-on with float tackle.

You must remember that despite their keen eyesight, pike also hunt by smell, especially the bigger pike that are often too lazy to chase smaller, live fish. Pike can only grow big as long as they convert more food into growth than they use up in energy to capture the food, and a large dead-bait that requires little energy to find and consume fits the equation better than does the chasing, killing and consuming of a number of small fish of the equivalent total weight.

Usually, therefore, a fairly large dead-bait, legered or laid on the bottom, is more likely to attract a big pike than is any other bait or method, although, of course, there are exceptions.

There is no necessity to use a whole fish. A half-bait

A pike of 24 lb 8 oz (11 kg), taken from Loch Lomond.

Pike are the traditional winter species, and they respond to a variety of fishing methods.

is often better because the juices that flow from the exposed insides permeate the water and serve as an added attractor. At one time, to enhance this juicy attraction, I injected dead-baits with fish oils and essences, but I never confirmed that it offered any great advantage, and now usually fish just a half-bait.

The tail half of a herring or mackerel are both very good, but for some reason there are waters where one or the other is very much preferred. To find out if one is better than the other for your water, fish two rods with a half-herring on one and a half-mackerel on the other until such time as the preference becomes clear.

An important difference between the two baits is that mackerel are much tougher fish than herring and can withstand casting to a much greater degree. For long-distance fishing, when power must be put into the cast, a mackerel is the obvious choice.

The bait should be attached with two treble hooks set about 3–4 in (7.5–10 cm) apart on the trace, a single point of each treble embedded firmly under the skin of the bait. The top treble should be positioned in the wrist of the bait's tail and the bottom treble at full stretch towards the severed end of the fish.

At close range it is not often necessary to use a leger weight, the weight of the fish on free-line tackle being sufficient. At long range a 1–2 oz (30–60 g) Arlesey bomb on a short link can be used. A float is not usually necessary to indicate bites, as pike more often than not pick up the bait and run with it for some distance. A coil of cooking foil or some other indicator on a loop of line between butt-ring and reel is perfectly adequate.

There are times, fortunately not too often, when pike pick up the bait and wolf it down on the spot. On leger tackle, especially on a free-line rig, they can do this without giving so much as a twitch on the indicator. For this reason, it is better to lay-on deadbaits with float tackle, for the float will give an immediate indication of any interference with the bait. The pike should be treated with as much respect as any other fish, and deep-hooking avoided at all costs. A float will be a great help towards this end.

The float should be set about 1 ft (30.5 cm) over-depth, the cast made, and the rod placed in two rests. Then the line should be tightened so that there is no slack between bait and float. The bale arm of the reel should be left open as a precaution against pike that dash off with the bait. Tension on the line can be maintained by looping the line under an elastic band on the rod butt, or under a plastic run clip specially designed for the purpose. These can be purchased from most angling suppliers.

The old-fashioned way of dealing with a pike run was to strike only after the first run had stopped and the second run had begun. It was thought that pike grabbed a victim side-on and ran with it. That it then turned the fish head-on and started to swallow it head first, and then ran again. To wait for the second run is a sure way of gut-hooking pike.

At the time this technique was recommended, it was common practice to take the catch home for the pot, so it did not affect the end result, which was a dead pike. Today the vast majority of dedicated pike anglers return their catch to the water in no worse condition than before they were caught. To do this, gut-hooking has to be avoided, which means that the 'second run' nonsense should be totally ignored.

The correct time to sweep the rod back and plant the hooks has to be judged from the experience you gain on the waters you fish, bearing in mind that there will be variations in the way the pike feed from one fishing session to the next. I always strike at the first positive movement of the indicator for the first two or three runs of a fishing session. If these runs are missed, then, and only then, will I allow some delay before striking. It is better to err on the side of the pike and miss a few, rather than delay for too long and gut-hook one pike.

When pike are making a noisy display of feeding, exploding at the surface as they lash their tails to produce a sudden burst of velocity, and pursuing their victims hard, it usually pays to float-fish a bait not far below the surface. The ideal bait for this is a sprat, and it need only be hooked with one treble through the root of the dorsal fin. Runs should be struck at immediately the float plunges beneath or travels across the surface.

I am not a great lover of spinning for pike, but I do admit that there are many occasions when it is the best method of catching them. It is also a good method for warming you up on a cold winter's day when there has been little or no action on dead-bait methods.

The short, whippy rods that are sold as spinning rods are not recommended. Although they are ideal for casting lures accurately, they lack the back-bone to plant the large hooks with which most lures are armed. An 11 ft (3.35 m) rod of at least 1¼ lb (0.55 kg) test-curve with a medium fast-taper action is much better. With such a rod, the hooks can be driven in quite adequately when it is bent into the butt. It is also better for playing bigger pike that have to be bullied away from weedbeds or other snags. The disadvantage of this longer and heavier rod is its less accurate casting ability, specially in confined areas, and the extra weight when spinning continuously over a long period.

A wire trace is just as essential when spinning as it is with any other pike fishing method. It should be at least 18 in (45 cm) long and attached to the line via a plain barrel swivel. A link-swivel should be tied to the other end so that lures can be changed quickly.

There are many different kinds of lures: leaf-like vanes that revolve round a central barrel, shaped and kinked lengths of metal plate that simply wobble; and the various plugs that either dive, pop across the surface, undulate, or make some other peculiar movements that are supposed to emulate the actions of a real fish. All of them are made in various sizes, shapes and colours. You can collect them, like some anglers collect floats, but you will probably end up with a few favourites that you use far more than all the others put together. Begin with your proven favourites, and if these fail to move any fish, ring the changes in the hope that the pike will respond to something you have in your collection.

The spinning technique is based on an attempt to emulate the actions of a real fish. It is not a matter of simply casting in and retrieving the lure in one fast, unbroken and straight line. The rod tip should be swung one way, then the other. The retrieve should be slowed down, or even stopped occasionally, to allow the lure to sink, then raise the tip to draw the lure towards the surface. Real fish swim in short bursts, sometimes slow, sometimes fast. Stricken fish, a favourite meal of pike, often swim to the surface, and flap there before slowly sinking. Think of this when you are spinning and make your lure imitate these actions as much as possible.

You should always have the right tools for unhooking pike, which is an easy operation if done correctly. The first requirement is a tough leather glove, which, if you are right-handed, is worn on the left hand. Lay the pike on its back and kneel astride it, holding the lower jaw open with your gloved hand. Next, you need a pair of long artery forceps or long-nosed pliers to grip and remove the hooks. If the pike is hooked in the throat, very carefully use the forceps through the gill, ensuring you don't damage the delicate gill filaments. Take your time, do not be frightened, and be positive. That way, the pike can be returned unharmed and may be even bigger the next time you catch it.

Coarse fishing on rivers

INTRODUCTION

Rivers, as far as this book is concerned, can be narrow streams; or the slow flowing, but wide and often deep, rivers like the Fenland drains; and those faster flowing, powerful rivers such as the Thames, Severn and the Hampshire Avon.

The vital difference between rivers and stillwaters as far as anglers are concerned, is the current. When choosing a swim, quite separate factors to those found in stillwaters have to be considered, as well as many of the various factors the two types of water have in common.

Rivers, however, have many advantages as well as disadvantages, not the least being that they generally produce fish far more consistently than lakes and pools. Although they are more difficult to fish in a practical sense, they are easier to fish as far as the fish being willing to feed is concerned.

SUMMER: BARBEL AND CHUB

The picture people have of a river in summer is of clear water, lush green plants that gyrate in the current, and the dark shapes of fish as they glide like ghosts across the gravel beds. That, however, is an apt description of a chalk bed river, such as the Hampshire Avon or Dorset Stour. Perhaps not as clean and lush as they were a couple of decades ago, but nevertheless considerably cleaner and clearer than the rain-fed rivers of the more northern regions.

Rivers in summer, whatever their type, are generally clear and settled, and in prolonged dry periods become low and weary looking. This is the time for stalking fish; wandering the river bank with the minimum of tackle and casting to fish as you spot them, rather than settling in one swim for the day.

Left Rivers in summer provide clear, and often low-water conditions; make use of the cover provided by bankside vegetation wherever possible.

Bankside vegetation will be at its densest and this should be used as cover whenever possible. Not only can you see the fish more easily in these clear, low-water conditions, but the fish can see you all the better too.

'Big baits for big fish' takes on a truer meaning with river fish in summer, for smaller fish such as minnows, gudgeon, bleak and dace are very active at this time of year, and small baits like maggots, if not taken properly by these tiddlers, are sucked until only skins remain. However, that does not mean you cannot use small baits, just that you have to accept the nuisance factor and be prepared to renew your bait far more often than usual.

For those anglers who like to get plenty of bites, regardless of the size of fish, tackle can be set to sink slowly, and swims primed to fever pitch with loose-fed maggots. Dace and bleak can be caught on every cast when a fine line, small hook and tiny bait such as a single maggot are used.

The low water conditions of summer inevitably mean that fewer swims will be available to the fish. This in turn means that it is more difficult for the angler to locate the fish. However, there is a silver lining to this particular cloud in that there are many more fish to a swim than usual. What it amounts to is that extra care, and perhaps some trial and error, is needed to find the fish, but once one of these 'hot-spots' is found, a large catch of fish is there for the taking.

Night-fishing, especially for barbel and chub, can be excellent on rivers in summer. When the river is extremely low and sluggish the fish very often refuse to feed at all in daylight, but wait for the dark and cooler nights. Many times it can be as though a switch has been thrown when darkness falls. An apparently barren swim will suddenly come alive and you can be active for most, if not all, of the dark hours, busily netting fish.

There is no doubt that one of the best river fish to try to catch in summer is the barbel. Not only does it feed actively throughout the summer months, but also, it is one of the best fighting fish, pound for pound, that swims.

Although barbel can be caught in winter, they are not nearly as easily caught as they are in summer. The same cannot so readily be said about other river species. For instance, the chub feeds almost as ravenously in winter as it does in summer, and although I enjoy an occasional session for summer chub, particularly with floating baits, and big natural baits like slugs, my true summer passion on rivers is the barbel.

Barbel

Barbel are long, slim, muscular fish, with barbuled, pointed snouts, big 'shoulders' and powerful fins. They have underslung mouths and tough, rubbery lips. One glance tells you that they are built for feeding on the bottom in strong currents, and when you hook one you realize just how tough and tenacious a scrapper they are. The grayling may be the 'Lady of the stream', but the barbel is no gentleman. Strong tackle and brute force are often the only way to dislodge it from its weedy quarters.

The barbel can grow well into double figures, but most fish in the rivers that are capable of producing more than the odd double-figure specimen, average around 6 lb (2.7 kg). At any size above 2 lb (0.90 kg) you know when you have hooked one.

Locating barbel can be a relatively simple business on the clear chalk streams with gravel bottoms. With the aid of polarizing spectacles you can walk along a stretch of river, stopping regularly to peer over the bankside vegetation and, once your vision becomes adjusted to the underwater scene, spot barbel as they nose over the gravel beds. On the murkier, rain-fed rivers, where gravel beds are not so common, and you

cannot so easily see the fish, you have to know what types of swim the barbel prefer.

Smaller barbel like the fast stretches, where the current races along at a fair pace and the depth is no more than about 5 ft (1.5 m). They gather in large shoals in such stretches, and if you like fast and furious sport, these are the swims to fish.

Bigger barbel prefer more sedate conditions. Although they still love to feel a current running over their backs, the swims they choose are invariably deeper and not quite so racy. More often than not, too, there will be a slacker pocket of water nearby where they can rest and where food collects, and offers comfortable feeding. And although it is not an absolute necessity, if the swim holds a snag, a sunken branch or tree, or a thick weedbed, then so much the better. Similar conditions can also be found where there is a pronounced dip, or basin, in the river bed.

The rod I use for barbel is 11 ft (3.35 m) long and has a test-curve of 1¼ lb (0.55 kg). Whereas I normally prefer a rod with an all-through action, my barbel rod is a medium fast-taper type, which is better for casting a fairly heavy swimfeeder accurately. It has a threaded tip-ring so that I can use a quiver-tip when necessary, although it rarely is.

My fixed-spool reel is filled with 6 lb (2.70 kg) line, but I have a spare spool that holds 8 lb (3.50 kg) line for bigger fish in especially snaggy areas.

There is no doubt that since the 1970s the swimfeeder, combined with either maggot or caster, has been the first choice with barbel anglers. Barbel tend to become preoccupied with a certain food, and the swimfeeder/maggot or caster combination is the best weapon to take advantage of this.

The swimfeeder is simply a plastic, perforated cylinder from 2 in (5.1 cm) to 3 in (7.6 cm) long and up

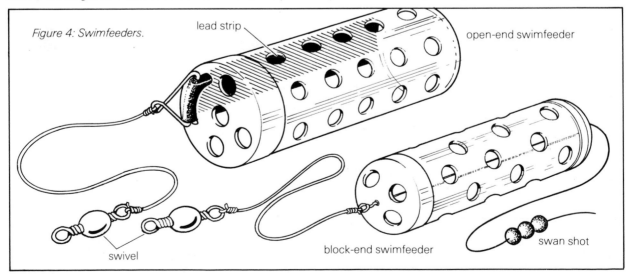

Figure 4: Swimfeeders.

lead strip

open-end swimfeeder

swivel

block-end swimfeeder

swan shot

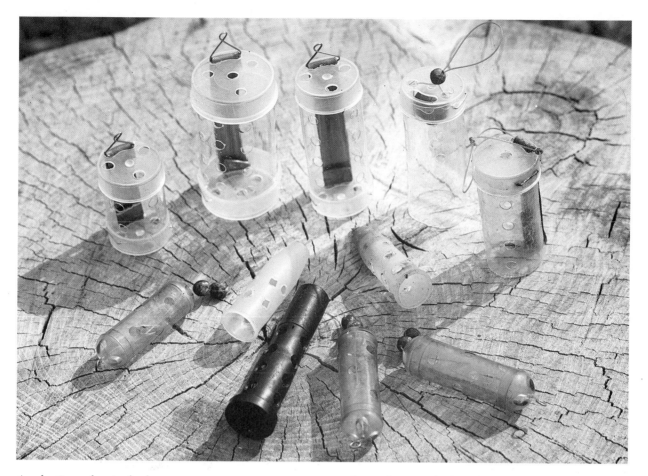

A selection of swimfeeders.

to about 1 in (2.5 cm) in diameter. It replaces the leger weight on the line and is filled with samples of the hookbait, usually maggot or caster or, the latest popular bait, a mixture of hemp and caster. There are two basic types of swimfeeder, the open-end and the block-end (see figure 4). The open-end is better with inert baits; you simply stop the ends with a plug of soft groundbait.

The procedure is to fill, cast, and allow the swimfeeder to empty into the swim as often as possible for the first half-hour or so after tackling up. What you are trying to do is attract fish into the swim, build their confidence, and cause them to become totally preoccupied with feeding on your hookbait, which will be creating a path of feed down the river. The important point is always to cast to the same spot so that there is only one line of feed leading to your baited hook. Inaccurate casting makes several lines of feed and so defeats the whole object of swimfeeder fishing.

Once the barbel have begun to feed in earnest, you can slow down on the frequency with which you fill

and cast the swimfeeder, though it is better to reduce the feed by only half-filling the swimfeeder, rather than reducing the rate of casting by too much.

Unfortunately, the barbel have become so educated to maggot and caster that it is essential to use a small hook, a size 14 being about the biggest you can get away with, but 16 and even 18 are often essential. Bigger hooks do not stop you from getting bites, and really good rod-bending bites at that. What happens, though, is that the barbel simply grab hold of the ends of the maggots or casters, without mouthing the hook, and pull hard. With a small hook they cannot do it so easily.

A reduction in line strength is not necessary. More often than not, a 6 lb (2.70 kg) main line and a 5 lb (2.25 kg) hook length is right, or when the fish are big and living close to tough snags, an 8 lb (3.50 kg) main line and a 7 lb (3 kg) hook length.

Inevitably, when the bigger barbel are hooked on small hooks, a few are lost, either through the hook bending or breaking, or simply because the tremendous pressure a barbel exerts causes the hook to lose its hold. If we could depend on every hook being perfectly made, and every hookhold ideal, then small

Night-fishing can be very productive in summer. Make sure that everything is laid out in advance.

hooks could cope. However, it is not like that in reality and the consequence is a lost fish.

It is doubtful whether any other bait than maggot, caster and hemp can have such a hypnotic effect on barbel, but it is certain that other, bigger baits, that allow bigger, stronger, and therefore safer, hooks to be used, are better for the bigger fish. One may not get as many bites, but each bite is more certain to be connected with, and the fish safely landed.

The noted and proven bigger baits for barbel are lobworms, cheese, bread to some extent, and meaty baits such as sausage meat paste and luncheon meat. Only in the last few years have I begun to experiment with the so-called particle baits, such as tares and sweetcorn, and they are showing great promise.

This search for a productive particle bait has been prompted by the need to capitalize on the deadliness of the swimfeeder/maggot method, without the handicap of using small hooks. Of course, a new bait will be successful only until the time when a great number of barbel anglers begin to use it and the barbel become as educated to it as they are now to maggots and casters.

Sweetcorn, and other particle baits, can be fished in a big, open-ended 'feeder. I use a size 6 hook crammed with as many as six grains of corn, and the barbel take it freely. That is, once they have homed in on the bait and become preoccupied with it. My pal, Ray 'McGinty' Beresford and I have had great success on the Hampshire Avon with sweetcorn fished in the way described, McGinty taking a 10½ pounder (4.8 kg) and myself catching half a dozen that included two over 9 lb (4 kg). I have also had some good catches on sweetcorn on the river Severn.

Whatever bait you use for barbel when legering,

An 11 lb 14 oz (5.3 kg) barbel taken from the River Wensum.

bites are usually quite vicious. The rod can be propped in the rest, lying completely motionless, apart from a slight tremble caused by the current, when very suddenly it will curve over fast, just as though a great weight has been dropped on the rod tip. Your rod should never be left unattended when fishing for any species, but with barbel it is especially dangerous, for your rod can be dragged into the river and never seen again.

Although I greatly favour the swimfeeder for barbel fishing, there are a few swims where it is better to fish a conventional link-leger. These are the extremely snaggy swims that contain sunken branches or jagged boulders; those swims where a swimfeeder is particularly prone to becoming trapped.

The link-leger should be a swan-shot type as in figure 5. This, if it does become trapped, will tend to have the shots stripped off it, freeing the tackle. It is also a very versatile leger weight in that shots can be added to or subtracted from the link according to the speed of the current and the weight required.

When fishing luncheon meat, or a similar bait with a plain link-leger, you have to introduce the loose feed by hand, or with a catapult if you are fishing a distant swim. The meat should be chopped up into bait-sized cubes and stored in a proper bait box before you go fishing. This way it is easier to feed a few cubes into the swim as you fish, and it avoids taking tins to the waterside with the risk of leaving them there. In fact, many angling clubs have banned the use of tins and insist that only genuine bait boxes are used.

Some luncheon meats, especially the fatty ones, tend to float, and while these are good enough for hookbait they are useless for loose feeding. It pays to check that the brand you have bought is the sinking kind before you set off for your day's fishing.

Luncheon meat, and other meat baits, can be fished on large hooks, even a size 2, where the barbel are not too fussy. I prefer smaller cubes and fish these on an 8 or 6 hook. My line strength remains the same whatever bait I use, but I tend to use a more through-action rod when I do not have the weight of a swimfeeder to cast.

A word of caution about cubed meat baits, however, specially the popular luncheon meat. On some waters the barbel have become wary of them, and I am sure much of their suspicion is aroused by the shape. For some time I noted a slight improvement when I cut the meat into different shapes, such as long oblongs and flat triangles, but this may have been no more than coincidence, in that the barbel were in a more co-operative mood on those days.

A striking improvement came about when I squashed the meat up into a soggy mass, and stiffened it with flour. I could mould this paste into any shape I fancied, and as it was a paste rather than a solid mass, the hooking power was improved, due to the hook being more easily struck through the bait.

Once you have caught a number of barbel from the same stretch on the paste bait, that too will become suspect, but now it is easy to alter the bait and allay their suspicions. All you do is mix in an oxo cube or two, either meat or chicken flavour. Or you can buy any of the concentrated flavours that carp bait suppliers sell. You can add almost anything to the basic luncheon meat-flour mixture, such as crushed hemp seed, powdered soups; anything edible, in fact, that can be found on supermarket shelves and that will make the bait 'different' for a while.

It is not very often I do so, for very few barbel swims lend themselves to it, but whenever I can I love to float-fish for this tremendously hard-fighting species. There

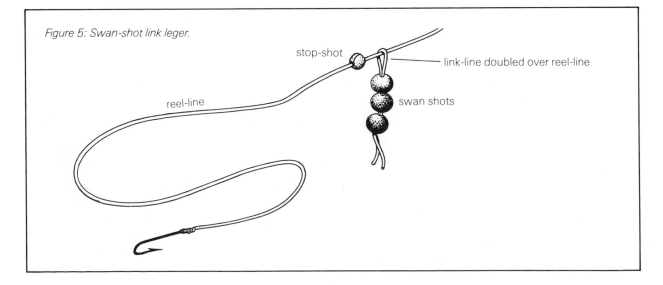

Figure 5: Swan-shot link leger.

stop-shot

link-line doubled over reel-line

reel-line

swan shots

is nothing quite like the thrill of seeing your float sink out of sight in a barbel swim, and knowing that when you strike it could be a most powerful force on the hook.

A 12 ft (3.65 m) or 13 ft (3.95 m) rod, with the power to cope with the species, would be ideal, but I manage with my 11 ft (3.35 m) legering rod. It hardly seems worth building one specially for the few occasions I am able to float-fish for barbel. The same strength of line, about 5 lb (2.25 kg) or 6 lb (2.70 kg) on your fixed-spool reel is right for the job.

I usually choose a smooth glide to trot down with my float tackle, using a large stick float for swims under my own bank, or a bodied waggler for more distant swims. The shots can be bunched about 1 ft (30 cm) from the hook in the faster swims, or spread down the line in the slower ones.

The swim can be fed by hand or catapult, but a more efficient method for close-in swims is with the use of a bait-dropper. This is a plastic container that you can use on your trotting rod or, better still, on a spare rod. You simply fill the container with hookbait, usually maggot or caster, and lower it to the bottom at the head of your swim. A triggering device; a lever, or a snatch on the rod tip opens the 'dropper and the contents spill out on the bottom of the river. It is a particularly useful device when there are nuisance species around, such as dace and bleak, rising to the surface to take loose feed that has been thrown in by hand. With a bait-dropper you know your free offerings are being distributed along the bottom, which is where the barbel are most likely to find them.

Never be afraid, however, to experiment. Although barbel are built for bottom feeding, they are not averse to feeding at any level, including the surface, if it suits them at the time. Float-fishing enables you to present the bait at various levels, and you would be wise to try these variations whenever there is little or no success with a bottom-fished bait.

Chub

Fishing for chub in summer often necessitates somewhat different tactics than one uses in winter. Natural baits, such as slugs and crayfish, come into their own, and, when the water is low and clear, stalking techniques using natural cover to sneak up and spot individual fish are effective.

In rivers where there are thousands of small chub for every big one, stalking can be the only way to catch the specimen. In a conventional situation, where you feed a swim and fish it for a long spell, it is rare indeed for the big fish to take your bait before the smaller ones. If you stalk the big fish, you can ensure that it is given a chance to take your bait before anything else does.

AUTUMN: ROACH AND DACE

I love rivers in autumn. At this time of year, from around the middle of September, to mid-December or so, rivers are at their best; providing, that is, the amount of rain we have is not excessive. Even then, however, if floodwater conditions are prolonged, and the fish become accustomed to the high water levels, sport can still be very good.

In the autumn period, the water temperature of rivers becomes more stable; there are few extremely hot spells and, as yet, not too many really cold periods. As a result, the fish establish themselves in specific swims and remain there for much longer than usual.

At this time of year the larders of natural food begin to run out and fish become more inclined to accept anglers' baits. Also, on the heavily coarse-fished rivers, where big fishing contests are held regularly, the fish have, by now, come to accept the popular baits like maggots and casters as natural, and there is very little problem in getting a shoal of fish feeding ravenously on a regular helping of loose feed.

Night fishing becomes less necessary, for the fish are more willing to feed in the daylight hours, although early morning and late evening remain the most productive periods. Float-fishing, or long-trotting, as it is known on rivers, comes into its own in autumn, for the minnows and sticklebacks are less of a nuisance, and the bigger river species have a better chance of taking the bait before it is stolen.

When heavy rain does cause the river to colour and exceed its normal level by several feet (metres), fishing is usually poor, but the lucky angler who discovers the slacks and backwaters where the fish hold up can make a killing.

Some rivers fish better than usual when the water level is just beginning to rise, and the water has only a tinge of colour. Other rivers fish better after a flood, during the period when the water level is falling and the colour clearing.

River fishing in autumn, however, is a sheer delight. When the leaves on the trees are all shades of gold and bronze and beginning to fall the river seems to come alive; just as though the fish are thinking: 'this is our last chance before winter sets in, let's have a good feed to see us through'.

River fishing in autumn is so good you can fish with absolute confidence for any species. They all feed very well at this time of year. I have decided, however, to tell you in some detail about roach and dace fishing; not because they are easier to catch, relatively speaking, than any other species at this time of year, but for the reason that they are both usually, and most efficiently, caught by long-trotting with float tackle.

Roach

Roach are the most popular coarse fish in Britain, and no doubt one of the reasons for this is that they are the most wide-spread. There are very few rivers that do not hold roach, as there are very few anglers who have not caught one or more.

In most rivers they rarely grow to more than 1 lb (0.45 kg) or so in weight, but there are a few exceptional rivers where they can exceed 2 lb (0.90 kg). Whatever weight they grow to, however, there is no denying that they are a pleasure to look at, with their silvery bodies and colourful fins, and an even greater pleasure to catch.

They are shoal fish, and the angler who is fortunate enough to find a shoal that lives along a gentle stream where trotting is easy, can expect to catch a good netful if he goes about it in the right way. Very rarely do you catch just one or two roach, unless they are those big, almost solitary fish. Catching one roach can mean there are plenty more to follow.

Roach, whether stillwater or river fish, feed best when the sun is off the water, and the light-level is poor. Dull, overcast days usually produce the better roach fishing, and the best time of all is late evening, when the light is fading fast.

And that is another reason why autumn is a good time to fish for them, for you can have a day on the river and fish until darkness, and still arrive home at a reasonable hour.

There is one thing in particular, apart from bright light, that roach do not like, and that is a soft, muddy river bed. They almost always look for clean sand and gravel to carpet their living quarters. And if there are nearby water plants such as cabbages (submerged lilies), or overhanging hawthorn or elder bushes to provide a roof, so much the better. Occasionally, and especially in summer, they can be found in fast water, but in autumn they prefer the more sedate, gentle swims, that flow steadily along at a slow walking pace. However, that is a general rule, and one should never ignore the possibility of some fish being found where least expected.

Most roach are found in swims that are ideal for swimming the stream with float tackle. The most useful rod for this type of fishing is a 12 ft (3.65 m) or 13 ft (3.95 m) match rod with most of its action in the top section. The new, light, carbon rods are the ultimate, but if your finances will only stretch to a glass-fibre rod there is no need to worry; I used one for

Left Chub and barbel will be found in the highly oxygenated water close to the weir.

years, as have thousands of other anglers, and caught plenty of roach.

Many anglers are reverting back to the old-style centre-pin reels for trotting. They are ideal for running a float through a swim in a steady, smooth, uninterrupted manner. However, far more skill is needed to use this type of reel, especially if you need to cast any distance, and it can take quite some time to become competent with one. Nevertheless, great pleasure is to be had with a centre-pin reel, and it is well worth persevering until you become proficient.

Having said that, thousands of anglers trot float tackle extremely skilfully with a fixed-spool reel, so the choice is a matter of personal preference.

The reel-line, for most swims, need be no more than 2½ lb (1.15 kg) breaking strain, with a hook length of 2 lb (0.90 kg) or even finer if the fish are not too big. On heavily fished rivers it may be necessary to fish with a 1 lb (0.45 kg) bottom to get bites, but such a fine line should only be used as a last resort, and only after you have become thoroughly skilled in handling reasonable fish on light tackle. It is always better to begin with an absolutely 'safe' line, and then gradually reduce this if it is necessary.

Most roach in rivers are caught on maggot or caster. Not necessarily because they are the best bait for the river roach, but because they are among the best baits for loose feeding and trotting. For this reason it is usual to use a size 18 hook, or even a 20 on heavily fished rivers. Indeed, it would be silly to use anything bigger than an 18 when it will be tied to a fragile line, for you could not sink in a bigger hook with the power you have available in a very light line.

The hook should be spade-end and fine in the wire for smaller roach. A forged and stronger variety is better for the bigger roach, to avoid the hook bending under pressure.

A selection of both stick and waggler floats is required to cover all the situations and swims you are likely to fish. The stick-floats, which are attached with a rubber at the top and bottom of the float, are needed for close-in work in reasonably calm conditions, and the wagglers are ideal for longer casting, especially when there is a downstream wind. A bodied waggler, well shotted, is necessary for those far bank, faster-flowing swims.

The shotting is very important. In the faster swims it is vital to get the bait down to the bottom quickly, otherwise you will be at the end of your trot before the bait is presented in the right area. This means that the bulk of the shot must be bunched down the line, with a final shot, or perhaps two shots, up to 9 in (22.85 cm) from the hook.

For those swims which are steady glides, that we can

Graham Marsden nets a roach.

fish with a stick-float, the shots should be spread down the line at regular intervals, beginning with the biggest shot nearest to the float, and then a shot of the next size down, 6 in (15 cm) below that, and the next smallest size of shot 6 in (15 cm) below that, and so on until it terminates with a dust shot no less than 6 in (15 cm) from the hook. Obviously, the depth of swim, the weight-carrying capacity of the float, and the distance you need to cast will all have a bearing on the ultimate number and size of shots used.

The aim is to present a bait that can be made to rise from the bottom in a natural manner. It is not always desirable to do this, but when it is, it can be deadly. This method is necessary when the roach are shoaled behind a natural rise in the river bed which swirls the loose feed upwards in the current, causing the roach to rise from the bottom to intercept the food. It can also be a deadly ploy where there is no rise in the river bed. By causing the bait to rise a few times while trotting down the run, you can spur the fish into grabbing it.

The way to cause the bait to rise from the bottom is by holding back the float against the natural flow. The longer you hold back the float, the higher the bait will rise. Once you have determined, by trial and error, how far from the bottom the fish are most inclined to take the bait, you can hold back the float for just the right length of time.

Occasionally, you can catch fish that are feeding off-bottom in a much more simple way by pushing the float down and allowing the bait to trot down at a constant distance from the bottom. However, more often than not, better sport can be achieved by allowing the bait to rise from the bottom just as loose feed does in a natural manner.

When the float is held back, any kind of shotting pattern will allow the bait to rise, but the 'tapered shot' method is the most efficient. It causes the line from float to hook to rise in an almost straight line, ensuring that you are in direct contact with the fish at all times and any bite will show immediately at the float. Most other types of shotting pattern might allow a degree of slack line, and bites would not be registered during some part of the lift.

There is no one more keen than I to catch a fish when I arrive at the waterside, but I curb my impatience for at least five to ten minutes and simply loose feed the swim, firing about a dozen maggots or casters to the head of the swim from a catapult every thirty seconds or so. A catapult is much better than throwing by hand as it keeps the feed in a more compact circle.

You could, of course, catch a roach without this preliminary feeding stint, but the idea is to get them feeding confidently before a fish is hooked. If a fish is hooked before they have their heads down, there is a danger of scaring off the rest of the shoal when the hooked fish transmits its fear. Fish feeding with a false sense of security tend to ignore their companions being hooked, simply because most of their senses are tuned in only to the food. The ten minutes or so spent feeding before fishing is almost always well worthwhile, not only with roach, but with chub, dace and other fish too. I have spent up to half an hour on this preliminary loose feeding when the quarry was chub with considerable success.

On rivers that hold big roach of 1 lb (0.45 kg) or more, bread flake can be a killing bait. Flake-fishing demands a bigger hook and slightly stronger line; a size 14 hook at least, but a 10 is often better still, attached to a line of 2½ lb (1.15 kg) or even 3 lb (1.35 kg) breaking strain.

In place of loose feed you use fine, pure bread groundbait, mixed so that it will sink to the bottom before breaking up, but not so stiff that it stays on the bottom in solid lumps. Extra special care should be taken to prevent overfeeding, for groundbait can be very filling and sport is soon ruined.

Hemp, tares, and small worms are also good roach baits although there are times on big-roach rivers when a huge lobworm is the most successful of all, particularly when there is some colour in the water and legering techniques are being employed.

The best time to catch big roach is at dusk and in the first hour of darkness. The deeper pools and undercut banks are the swims to look for, but any deeper-than-average, slow-flowing swim is worth a try.

There are a few swims where a Betalight float can be used. This is a float with a gas-filled capsule built into the tip which glows in the dark. However, they do not burn brightly enough until full darkness has fallen; at dusk, they cause eyestrain at the expense of missed bites.

For this short two-hour spell it is better to leger, and for this you will need a 10 ft (3.05 m) to 11 ft (3.35 m) rod, a 3 lb (1.35 kg) reel-line, and a 2½ lb (1.15 kg) hook length. A quivertip with a Betalight fixed to the end can be used as an indicator, or you could hold the line and feel for bites. Bread flake or small cubes of crust on a size 10 hook are good, or worm when the water is coloured. Feed with groundbait, several pinches of squeezed flake, or a few worms flicked into the swim every ten minutes or so.

The best end-tackle is a swan-shot link-leger (figure 5) stopped 1 ft (30.5 cm) from the hook when flake or worm is the bait, or 2 in (5 cm) from the hook when the bait is crust. You should use just enough swan-shot to hold bottom in the swim you are fishing.

If you have decided that feeling for bites – or touch-legering, as it is popularly known—will be best for you, the rod should be positioned so that it points as directly as possible at the bait. Such a position will eliminate friction over the tip ring.

If, on the other hand, you decide to use a quivertip, there are two basic positions. The first is to sit so that the line runs at 90°, or thereabouts, from the rod, so that the full effect of the quivertip is utilized. The rod also points towards the surface of the river and all the line, except for the last few inches, is submerged. The second way is to prop the rod on a rod-rest so that the quivertip is high above the water.

The first method is better for swims that lie along your own bank. The second method is best for swims from mid-river to the opposite bank, for with the rod held or propped high plenty of line is out of the water, therefore not under the influence of the current, so less lead is needed to hold bottom. You should also consider the background, even in daylight, as the formation of some trees, or sunlight or moonlight shining through them, can make it very difficult to keep careful watch on the quivertip. Often, bites from roach at night can be very decisive, the quivertip wrenching round in one swift movement, but there are times when you have to react to the merest flutter.

Dace

Almost exactly the same tackle as that described for roach fishing is perfectly suitable for dace. The only exception is that dace are inclined to come up from the bottom and feed at, or near to, the surface far more often. A slight adjustment to the shotting, producing a slower-sinking bait is all that is necessary.

If you think it necessary, you can also reduce the line strength very slightly, for dace are generally smaller than roach and can often be very fickle, particularly when feeding near to the surface.

The major difference between roach and dace fishing on the river is that roach dislike strong light, whereas dace feed very actively when the sun is shining brightly. Not exclusively so, however, for the evening period when the sun drops below the horizon can be good too.

There is a distinct similarity in the type of swims that roach and dace prefer, but whereas roach will often tuck well into the bank, specially where it is undercut, dace prefer the more open water.

Smaller dace love streamy swims, particularly where a smooth glide of fairly deep water gradually breaks onto shallower water. The shelf where the river bed begins to rise, right down to the fast, streamy section is the hot-spot. A bait trotted down such a swim, with the float held back so that it rides up the shelf, can be a very effective method to use.

Again, maggot and caster are the best baits, with bread flake being *par excellence* for big dace, although there are times, such as in coloured-water conditions, when a small redworm is deadly.

Dace can be the most simple fish to catch most of the time, but there are occasions when they can be most frustrating. One of those times is when, on a hot, sunny day, you have loose fed the swim with maggot or caster and the dace are responding extremely favourably. So much so, that they have followed the stream of bait up to its source and are quite literally waiting for the next handful to hit the surface. I have lost count of the number of times this has happened to me, only to find that the dace quite willingly grab and consume the free offerings but very skilfully avoid the bait with a hook in it.

Obviously, they have noted the subtle difference in the rate at which the bait sinks; that the maggot or caster with a hook in it falls that tiny bit faster than those without. Every so often, a fish will still accept it, but even then the bite is usually fast and it spits it out quicker than you can strike.

The only thing to do is to make your hook-bait sink

Left *Winter on the river.*

Right *A handsome 5 lb (2.25 kg) chub.*

at the same rate as the loose feed. And this is where your fish-playing skill is severely tested, for you have to go down to a size 22 hook, or even a 24, and a 1 lb (0.45 kg) line, and be adept enough to persuade the fish to swim away from the shoal when hooked so that the rest are not frightened off. You will lose a few fish through poor hooking and you will still miss quite a number of bites, but it is great fun.

WINTER: CHUB

Snow and ice, bitter winds, fog, and rotting leaves that foul lines and sicken fish are all part of the winter scene on the river, each and every one a sound enough reason to stay at home with a hot toddy in front of a warm fire.

In spite of these conditions, I love fishing rivers in winter. There are many magic moments to savour, even in the face of such dispiriting weather, if you equip yourself properly, not only with the right tackle, but also with the right clothing. And there are many beautiful winter days, when the sun shines and it is no more than crisply cool.

I have had some excellent catches of fish in winter when snow has been falling around me in thick clouds and cat-ice has been chattering in the margins. I have also had many a poor day's fishing in winter when there has not been a snowflake in sight and not a sign of frost and ice. It is not only the prevailing conditions that have an influence, but also the preceding conditions. If there have been several days of ice and snow, the fish have had time to adapt and will feed despite the conditions, but sudden changes, even changes for the better, are usually bad news for a day or two.

The autumn fall of leaves can be a problem. In certain stretches where debris is most likely to accumulate, huge mounds of leaves rot and sour the water for some distance downstream. These leaves also gradually break away from the mound, specially during periods of high water levels, and foul anglers' lines.

Legering in these areas can be a nightmare, and the only recourse is to float-fish so that your line is travelling downstream at the same pace as the leaves. Where this problem is at its worst, the best solution is to avoid the areas altogether.

On the brighter side, the naked trees and the vast reduction in underwater vegetation allow access to swims which were unfishable in summer and autumn. Higher than normal water levels change useless or mediocre swims into good ones, and on the right day, when the fish are hungry, with little natural food on which to feed, anglers' baits are more than ever welcome.

It is becoming more obvious, as each season passes, that practically any species can be caught over the winter period if the angler is determined enough and persistent enough. Even barbel are no longer safe, for many anglers catch a few every winter. It should be noted, however, that the conditions in which the recognized summer species will feed in winter, are very limited. That is why chub are a better bet for the winter angler along the river.

Winter is a good time to catch chub because they are often the only fish that will feed. Even on the most bitterly cold day the odds are that one or two chub, somewhere, can be persuaded to take a bait. In good conditions, on the larger rivers where huge shoals of chub are found, nets of 40 lb (18 kg) and more are not unusual.

Chub are the pigs of the river, in that they eat anything and everything, and they have mouths to match; great cavernous holes ever open for an easy meal. At times, because of this ravenous appetite, they can be the easiest fish of all to catch, but there are other occasions when you have to use all the subterfuge at your disposal.

Chub can be found in most types of swim, but there are some which they are particularly partial to, and it is these we should make it our business to find. On the large, slow rivers that glide sedately through the countryside with little or no change of pace, it is a question of trial and error, for there is little visual evidence to help you to choose one swim from another. The large, slow rivers are, however, the most popular with match anglers, and it is a question of keeping your eyes and ears open and discovering from which area the winning weight usually comes from.

Apart from trial and error and match results, the only other way of taking at least some of the guesswork out of swim selection, is to plumb the depths carefully and find where there is some character to attract chub, such as slight obstructions and weedbeds that would trap food that comes down with the current. Also, look for the more streamy runs where the current ever-so-slightly quickens its pace.

On the smaller rivers that twist and turn every which way, the task of swim selection is considerably easier. There is so much character in them that the choicest swims are obvious, once you know what to look for. The smooth glides that have tree branches and bushes overhanging them; beneath the rafts of debris that collect on branches that protrude into the water; and the undercuts where the current has gouged into the river bank, particularly where this exposes tree roots: such swims are loved by chub, and there are usually many of these swims on a winding river.

Contrary to popular belief, chub are not particularly hard-fighting fish as compared, weight for weight with, say, barbel. The main fight of a chub is in its initial rush to escape when it feels the hook drive home. After that it slows down considerably and the angler has little difficulty keeping it under control.

For this reason, you should use a soft-actioned rod that will give easily to that initial surge. One of 11 ft (3.35 m) and 1 lb (0.45 kg) test-curve for legering is ideal. And a 13 ft (3.95 m) match rod is best for float-fishing.

Lines will be variable from 1½ lb (0.70 kg) to 8 lb (3.50 kg). That might seem a very wide range for the same fish, but each extreme is necessary at times, and each is used only in exceptional circumstances, as will be explained later. And again, with a range of hooks needed from a tiny size 20 to a big size 2, an explanation will be forthcoming.

The methods that can be used to catch chub are infinite, for they will feed at any level between bottom and surface and accept, depending on the day, a miniscule bait, or a massive one.

If there are shoals of chub, and the swim is suitable, such as a long, slow glide of fairly constant depth, long-trotting with float tackle will probably be the most productive method. Long-trotting also demands the most skill, for as well as the angler needing dexterity in tackle manipulation just to present a bait successfully in a natural manner throughout the whole course of the swim, he also has to be able to handle any large chub on the light tackle that is required to long-trot efficiently.

The match rod of 13 ft (3.95 m) should be used with a fixed-spool reel (or a centre-pin if you so wish) and a line of 2½ lb (1.15 kg). To begin with, a hook length of 2 lb (0.90 kg) should be tried, but you may find that more bites will develop if this is reduced to 1½ lb (0.70 kg) after a few fish have been hooked.

There is no doubt that a 5 lb (2.25 kg) reel-line and a 4 lb (1.80 kg) bottom would catch a chub or two at first, but it would be surprising if any more were caught on that tackle from the same swim. Chub are very crafty in that once one or two of their shoal-members have been hooked and they become spooked, they are quite capable of picking out the loose feed from the hooked baits. They can do this because a hookbait on a heavy line has no chance of behaving in the same way as loose feed, and the chub can spot the difference. By gradually reducing the strength and hook size they can be fooled.

But on a cold winter's day not many anglers want to be reducing line strength and hook size regularly over the first hour or two of fishing, so the answer is to begin the fishing session with relatively light line, with scope to make one change lighter if necessary.

Playing large fish on light tackle is a matter of confidence. If you go at it like a bull in a china shop, you have no chance, because any fish fights only as hard as the angler forces it to. The harder you pull at a fish, the harder it will pull back.

If you are fishing in or close to snags, you have no choice but to fish heavy, for you have to pull the fish away from the snag, which causes the fish to try to dig deeper into it. On the other hand, you cannot afford to be gentle because it is very unlikely that the fish will swim away from the snag of its own accord.

In relatively open water you can be gentle, and that is the way to play big fish on light tackle. All that is necessary is to maintain a tight line to stop the hook falling out, and at times, while constantly holding the rod high, gently to pressurize the fish, to guide it—not pull it—towards the landing net. The landing net should be submerged and still, so that the fish is not frightened in the final stages, causing it to bolt off.

With extremely light line and a hook perhaps as small as a size 20, you cannot rely entirely on the reel's slipping clutch mechanism. They are just not that efficient in the low tension range. What you have to do is set the clutch to give you as much safety margin as possible, but play the fish by backwinding when line has to be given. Those anglers who advocate that only the clutch should be used as a failsafe mechanism, obviously have not attempted to catch a big fish on light tackle. Once you have mastered the art of playing fish with the back-wind method, you will not use anything else, except in rare instances when fishing for big, fast-swimming fish with heavy line.

I will not go into any great detail about the trotting technique, for this is well covered in the roach fishing section. The only significant difference is in the amount of loose feed, in that several pints of maggots or casters are necessary for a day's fishing for chub in a productive swim, instead of the one or two pints that are usually sufficient for roach.

Another good way of chub fishing is to travel light, with only the bare essentials of tackle, and wander along the river bank taking an odd chub or two from every likely swim. This is one way of catching a large chub, for at times they are solitary fish and when you are aiming to pull only one or two from each swim you can afford to fish heavy.

I use an 11 ft (3.35 m) rod of 1¼ lb (0.55 kg) test-curve fitted with a quivertip. The fixed-spool reel is filled with 6 lb (2.70 kg) line and tied direct to a size 6 hook. The terminal tackle is a simple fold-over swan-shot link-leger as illustrated in figure 5.

There is a good reason for using this simple but very effective link-leger. It enables you to change its weight easily and quickly to suit each type of swim. It is a simple matter of adding or subtracting swan-shot according to the strength of the current. I do not, of course, have to use swan-shot; a smaller AA or BB shot can be used to make subtle changes.

For bait, I rarely use anything other than bread, in either crust or flake form, although I sometimes carry a box of lobworms and a wad of cheese paste if the water is coloured and a likelihood exists of the chub preferring these baits.

The way I approach this wandering style of chub fishing is to walk the whole length before casting a line, throwing a couple of handfuls of soaked bread into each likely swim. Then I return to the first swim I baited and begin fishing, knowing that the mashed bread will have given any chub in the area a taste of my hookbait and, with a little luck, an urge to nose around and look for more. The idea is to instil some confidence into them before the baited hook is presented.

The first swim may be a rubbish raft that juts out from my own bank; a twig and a leaf-strewn patch that could also be decorated with one or two empty beer cans and several bottles. In fact, rubbish rafts are just that; a collection of debris that has accumulated around a branch that brushes the river's surface. They are first-class holding spots for chub, for there is no doubt that these fish love a roof over their heads.

An experienced angler can look at the swim and have a very good idea how much weight is required, otherwise an experimental cast or two is necessary, bearing in mind that a crust, because of its built-in buoyancy, will need a little more lead than a piece of flake of similar size.

Too little lead and the bait will be dragged too quickly beneath the raft and tight into the bank. Too much lead and the bait will drop almost straight to the bottom, and will not roll under the raft at all. The aim is to use just enough lead to hold bottom when you cast to within a yard (metre) or so of the raft and then, with an occasional flick of the rod tip, be able to coax the bait to roll under the raft and come to rest exactly where you want it.

When flake is the bait, the link-leger should be stopped about 12 in (30.5 cm) from the hook. For crust this distance should be reduced to no more than 2 in (5 cm), for the buoyancy of crust will cause it to rise off bottom, and a rise of more than 2 in (5 cm) would be too much in normal circumstances.

If a quiver-tip is being relied upon as a bite-indicator, the rod should be positioned so that it points across the river and slightly downstream. You should sit facing the same way, with your fingers curled around the rod-butt and reel-seat, with your arm resting along your thigh, and with the weight of the rod supported with a single rod-rest about mid-way. You are then in an ideal position to see and strike at bites.

If you prefer touch-legering, that is, looping the line over a finger and feeling for bites, then your position should be altered a little so that you point more downstream, and the rod points directly at the bait.

There is not usually long to wait for a bite in these rubbish-raft swims. If the chub are there and willing to feed, you should get a response within minutes of casting. Indeed, when employing this wandering style of chub fishing, never spend more than twenty minutes or so in any one swim without a bite of some description. If there is a bite, and you fail to hook it, then it is worth spending a little more time, experimenting with hook and bait size, and different baits, to see if you can get a more positive take. Otherwise, move on and try the next swim.

One swim you might come across could contain a sunken tree, whose branches create a heavily-snagged area, where the chub love to reside. Or it could be a deeply undercut bank beneath a tree whose roots are exposed, which also offers a much-loved sanctuary to chub. Whichever, it means that tough tackle is needed to remove the chub from these snags, for it is necessary to fish right amongst the branches or roots to get the best out of the swim, and the biggest fish if any are there, for they do not wander far from these 'safe' areas. This is where the 8 lb (3.50 kg) line becomes a must, with a hook no smaller than a size 6; the set-up and bait remain the same.

The technique is to cast as close as possible to the snags and then allow the current to carry the bait right into the thick of it. The rod should be held at all times and the reel's clutch set tight so that no line is given.

When a bite is registered—and the bites in these swims are usually vicious and rod-thumping—the rod should be swept back and held with a full bend into the fish. With luck the chub will kick just once and then pop out of the snags like a cork out of a bottle. From there you play the fish in a conventional manner, ensuring that it is not allowed to turn and dash back into the snags. Do not, during that first strike into the chub, give any line whatsoever, for you have already given some when you took up the bend in the rod. Sometimes, even that is enough to allow the chub to wrap your line around a branch or root.

There are, of course, many winter days when the conditions are so severe that even chub are difficult to tempt. During these times, the same tactics can be used as already described, but it will be necessary to reduce the hook and bait size and to cut down, even eliminate, the use of groundbait and loose feed. The use of a quivertip in such conditions is highly recommended, for it will be too cold to touch-leger and any bites could be very feeble. Although you probably will not catch many fish, to catch one is supremely satisfying when the odds are so much against it.

PART II
TROUT FISHING

Trout fishing on stillwaters

Trout fishing on rivers

Trout fishing on stillwaters

INTRODUCTION

Fishing for trout in stillwaters throughout Britain must be the largest growth industry in field sports in recent years. The types of water available to the flyfisher vary considerably in size, quality and cost and there is now a water containing trout within striking distance of all flyfishers. The quality of trout fishing may not always be to the liking of everyone, but by being selective it is usually possible to achieve a happy medium and everyone now has their favourite water.

The earlier form of trout fishing on stillwaters started with water authority reservoirs which had previously been used solely for supplying drinking water. They were then utilized for sports, and stocked with trout in some instances; such waters which spring to mind are Hollowell and Ravensthorpe, both close to Northampton, and Blagdon near Chew. Sadly, both Ravensthorpe and Hollowell are classic examples of a slip-up in management because both waters, having in their hey-day been capable of producing very large brown trout, were invaded by coarse fish. Although perch and roach fry feed up cannibal trout very nicely, the pike that also found their way into the waters thrive superbly on stock-sized trout. Some very heavy pike now populate Hollowell, which has ceased to be a trout fishery as such, as did Ravensthorpe until it was drained and divested of the pike in recent years. It is fair to say that although all large stillwaters, and a good number of small ones, contain a large head of coarse fish, the commercialization of the sport in recent times has meant that fishery managements now appear to be keeping abreast of the problem on almost every water.

Naturally, the small waters are easier to manage, and with the explosion of fishing for trout in reclaimed gravel pits and newly-dug pits or flooded land, most are now built with the intention of emptying them when required exactly for the purpose of controlling any coarse fish, and also of course for monitoring the stocking of the water with trout.

When talking of a large stillwater it must be remembered that reservoirs have been built in Britain at a fairly fast rate since 1945, and whereas a water of just over, say 100 acres was at one time large, it is now a pygmy among stillwaters when compared to waters such as Rutland and Kielder, which are in excess of 3000 acres. Again, by stark comparison the small stillwaters such as Avington, Church Hill Farm and Stafford Moor, which were constructed especially for the stocking and catching of trout, have entirely fishable banks around just a few acres of water.

Because these smaller waters rely wholly on the fishing for their existence—they are put-and-take fisheries, which means that they are stocked on a more regular basis than the large ones—it is common for them to be re-stocked at least once a day. Another feature almost exclusive to small waters is the tendency to stock them with trout of a larger size, therefore the fishing may be that much more expensive. They usually have their own stew ponds on site in which small fish are grown on to varying sizes, and most of the smaller stillwaters now boast trout of immense proportions which at one time were only dreamt of in this country.

Because of the vast number of fish required to stock a large water to make it worthwhile fishing, the fish introduced tend to be smaller, unless the water authority is seeking unwarranted publicity. However, by virtue of the size and depth of a large water, the fish escape capture, at least the more fortunate ones do, for a longer period of time and therefore will grow on naturally and tend to be more edible than those from a small water. They also become very select in their feeding habits; a large fish from a water such as

Above right *Three fishermen have struck lucky in this area of open water where they have located a concentration of rainbow trout.*

Right *Wading may be unavoidable on large waters. Cast into the shallows close to the bank before entering the water in case fish are lying close in.*

Above *When casting in a high wind, you will have to adapt your technique to cope with the conditions.*

Below: Left column, top to bottom: *Damselfly Nymph number 1, Damselfly Nymph number 2, Sedge Pupa number 3, Sedge Pupa number 1, Sedge Pupa number 2.* Middle column, top to bottom: *Sedge Larva number 1, Sedge Larva number 3, Sedge Larva number 2, Pond Olive Nymph, Pheasant Tail Nymph, Claret Nymph, Shrimp.* Right column, top to bottom: *Black Midge Pupa, Red Midge Pupa, Pale Green Midge Pupa, Olive Midge Pupa, Golden Dun Midge Pupa, Orange/Silver Midge Pupa, Phantom Midge Pupa, Fluorescent Red Midge Pupa, Fluorescent Green Midge Pupa.*

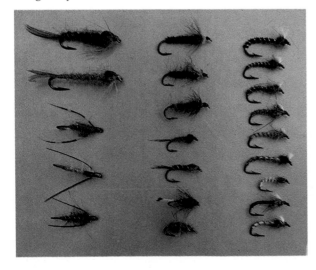

Grafham, Bewl Bridge or Sutton Bingham tends to be rated as more worthy of capture and will invariably, if it is in fine condition, be a much more handsome fish.

There is a vast difference in the tackle required to fish two waters such as Grafham and Avington, to provide two classic examples of opposite ends of the spectrum. Avington is a system of three small lakes fed by the river Itchen in Hampshire. The water is gin-clear and it is possible to cast almost to the opposite bank. The current world record rainbow trout came from Avington. Because it is in a sheltered valley, the wind is not usually a great problem. On the other hand Grafham is situated in flat country on the edge of the Fens near Cambridge in East Anglia and a moderate wind will always provide conditions which are uncomfortable unless the necessary tackle and clothing is being used. Also, it does not have any sheltered bays as such, so the only way to escape the wind is to be on the windward shore. It is really a 1600-acre saucer, and a large fish from this water is a difficult proposition because often it is 'blind' fishing, whereas in the clear waters of Avington the fish can be observed and stalked. This obviously requires lighter tackle than Grafham, where distance can sometimes make all the difference. This is not to say that all of the larger waters require heavy tackle and are difficult to fish. Indeed, such waters as Pitsford, Bewl Bridge and Ladybower are several hundred acres in size and yet their irregularity provides many sheltered bays which can be treated in the same way, almost, as a small water would be. At the end of the day, the water, the fishing and the tackle to be used are entirely at the discretion of the individual, and it is this that makes flyfishing so enjoyable.

The type of fishing preferred dictates the choice of tackle in every instance. There are light line outfits which are admirable for fishing over short distances and water of no great depth, and on a light line outfit the most sensible type of flyfishing would be dry fly or nymph. On a large blustery water, a heavier outfit may be necessary, but it is still possible to fish comparatively finely with a longer rod. The heavy lines and rods are really only essential for sinking-line fishing where a longer line needs to be cast and a heavier fly or lure is used.

Basically most waters can be fished with either sinking or floating lines, and almost without exception, or at least with very few exceptions, nymphs and dry flies are fished on floating lines and more usually so are wet flies, although nymphs and wet flies can be fished most effectively on a sunk line. Lures are more usually fished on a sinking line but, once again, can be most effective fished slowly on a floating line.

To classify the types of flies available is fairly simple. A dry fly is one that sits on the surface of the water or in the surface film; a nymph is an imitation of a water creature or insect, such as a freshwater shrimp or a hatching fly. A wet fly is one that is fished beneath the surface of the water, and is usually an imitation of a fly which has hatched; sedge fly imitations are a classic example, but some wet flies imitate nothing whatsoever and are merely bright or gaudy things designed to provoke aggression in the fish and are called attractors. Lastly, the lure is a larger fly, usually tied on long-shank hooks, and may be a representation of a small fish or simply a large attractor-type fly. In all cases, the flies used in fly fishing are tied with natural or artificial materials, such as hair, fur and feathers, and the only time a natural insect may be used is when the rules of the fishery allow it and then will almost certainly only be during the mayfly and crane fly (daddy-long-legs) periods.

The lines used to cast the fly are designated an AFTM number, which indicates their actual weight, and the type of line is also designated by initials. The higher the AFTM number of a line, the heavier it is. A light line would be classified as AFTM 4 or AFTM 5. Once a line gets over AFTM 9 it is becoming heavy, and it should only be necessary to go as high as AFTM 10 under the roughest of conditions or for some other reason peculiar to the user. The use of lines above AFTM 9 is more usually confined to salmon fishing and tournament casting. In recent times, the heavier lines have tended to be reduced to shooting heads (shooting tapers), meaning that instead of being a full-length line it is a shortened line with a light backing line, which

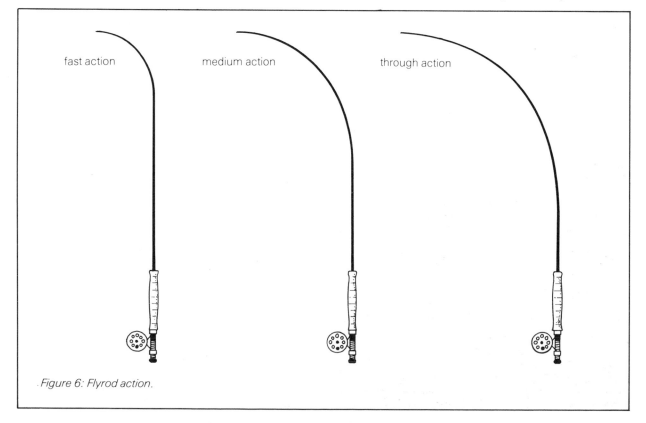

Figure 6: Flyrod action.

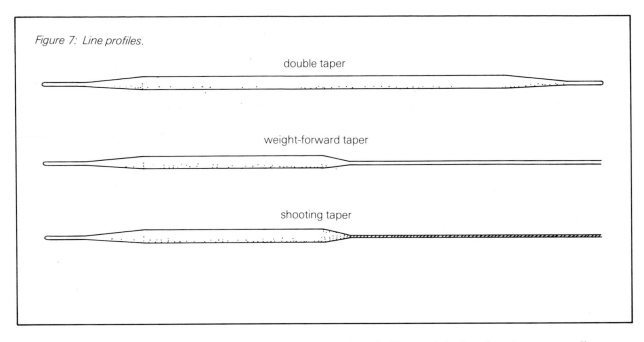

Figure 7: Line profiles.

double taper

weight-forward taper

shooting taper

theoretically means that the user should be able to cast further. Although the shooting head has the advantage that, used in the correct way, it is possible to cast further, the disadvantages of delicate presentation not being possible and accuracy being forfeited over further distances, definitely outweigh the single one of distance under most conditions. Shooting heads are best used as sinking lines for lure fishing.

The initials used to classify the type of line are: DT−double taper; WF−weight forward; ST−shooting taper.

An F(floating) or an S(sinking) tells whether the line will sink or float, and thus a line designated AFTM 6 WFF will be a floating weight-forward line of medium weight (6), which is excellent for fishing almost any water at surface level. There is also a sinktip line which is a floating line with a sinking tip at the forward end. These are weight-forward lines and can be very useful, although if they are not balanced properly, presentation becomes clumsy and they are not easily cast with accuracy, and such a line could be outfished with a slow sinking line or a floating line with a weighted fly. Sinking lines also have their own particular sinking rate; they can be slow, medium, or fast, and rates of sinking can vary between manufacturers. There is now an intermediate line available which has a virtually imperceptible sinking rate and is used for fishing a wet fly or nymph (and occasionally a lure) when there is no wind to ripple the surface and a floating line would create wake.

The line is weighted in order to flex the rod, and if it is likely that all sorts of water will be fished it would be best to consider the rod and line together. It is very difficult to define which is the more important, but the rod probably just has the edge. On very small waters, an 8 ft (2.45 m) rod is ideal, and should accommodate a line of 4 or 5 AFTM. When purchasing a line to match the rod, you must remember that a DT has a once-removed, correspondingly lower AFTM number than a WF and twice removed from ST. Thus a DT 7 will flex a rod to the same degree as a WF 8 and a ST 9. For boatfishing stillwaters a rod of at least 10 ft (3.05 m) should be employed, and with the introduction of modern materials much longer rods are possible without the disadvantage of increased weight. For ordinary bank fishing under all sorts of conditions a rod of 9 ft 6 in (2.90 m) is the best optimum length, and the line weight that would suit all conditions (which is always marked on the rod) would be shown as AFTM 6/7/8 or 7/8/9. This means that the rod will cast a DT 6, WF 7 and ST 8, and so on. Either one of these line classes would suit any condition on a 9 ft 6 in (2.90 m) rod, but the former would be better suited to calmer conditions or shorter distances than the latter.

Each type of line has a specific characteristic, the shooting taper is used mainly for distance, the double taper is used generally for casting accurately and delicately to fish at close quarters, and the weight forward combines the advantages, to a degree, of both. The great advantage of the WF is that it is possible to change direction much more quickly whilst false casting, which means that more rising fish can be covered.

Lastly, but of no less importance, is the leader, or tippet. This is the light, monofilament line which connects the line to the fly and therefore the thickness and length of the leader has a direct bearing on the presentation and ultimately the acceptance of the fly by the trout. It is possible to purchase tapered leaders, which theoretically means that at the delivery of the cast the fly rolls forward of the line. A level leader may not present the fly so well as a tapered one every time, but in the right hands the disadvantage is not noticeable, and the level leader is far less expensive and more convenient.

In every instance the choice of tackle and the amount, regardless of choice of venues, must be decided by the budget of the individual. Although on the whole 'you do get what you pay for', this is not always the case. It tends to be truer of lines than rods, but in experienced hands a glass fibre rod will perform just as well as a much more expensive carbon fibre rod.

SPRING

There is no such thing as still water where there is variable temperature, wind speed and direction. These factors are constantly affecting the movement of the water, and regardless of the size of the water, there will be some movement caused by wind or stratification. With these factors in mind, before the start of every trout fishing expedition, the water should be considered objectively and the recent wind and air temperatures taken into account. This is particularly important during the earliest months of the season, when the winter winds have had the opportunity of chilling the water, affecting the growth of weed and slowing down the cycle of the inhabitants of the water which the trout rely on for food.

The water temperature will be lower than it would be during the warmer months and this affects the trout in two very important ways due to their cold-bloodedness. Firstly, they will not be roaming as far or as fast, and secondly, they will be less willing to chase a fly which is being fished fast. All fish are living machines which convert food into energy in order to provide themselves with the ability to continue to catch more food. They require less food in cooler water and so require less energy. The trout does not attack for the sake of it, but does so either for food or for territorial reasons. With this in mind the reason for fishing slowly in water that is certainly cold can be clearly seen. Any sudden changes in water temperature will affect the willingness of the trout to feed, and this applies to both the upward and downward fluctuations in temperature. A drastic change will send the fish off the feed.

In the early months of the season, then, it stands to reason that the fish will be in the warmer layers of the water and the banks of any water that is affected by the wind will be holding fish on the leeward bank, and to a lesser degree the windward bank. Another reason

for this may be that the wave action will oxygenate the water on the leeward bank and fish will collect there for that reason. Unfortunately, these fish, mainly rainbow trout, may be out of condition, due to spawning. They should be avoided because they will be discoloured, emaciated, inedible and lacking fight: all in all, a fairly unsporting proposition, and they should be left to regain better condition.

At this time of the season, the better fish tend to be nearer the bottom unless the weather has been exceptionally warm and the ones that may be taken near the surface will probably be the ones that have recently been introduced.

To catch the fish that are in better shape and probably over-wintered, a slow retrieve is essential, and either a large nymph or a small lure is ideal. A floating line with a heavy or weighted fly, or alternatively a sinking line, will be needed to fish through the water until fish are located. It is a fair bet that fish will be gathered close to the leeward bank or in a corner which is leeward. If there are two banks funnelling floating debris into a deep corner, it is certain that fish will gather under the raft of rubbish that collects there. In these circumstances, the nymph or lure should be cast across the wind and towards the other bank, and by fishing slowly across the corner of the bay some fish should result. To retrieve the fly quickly will result in either out-of-condition fish or no fish at all.

With regard to the choice of rod, the early season is the one time when a carbon fibre rod has a distinct advantage over a glass fibre rod. When fishing into a strong wind, the relatively low diameter of the carbon rod meets with considerably less wind resistance than its glass counterpart, and therefore is less tiring to use. Coupled with the fact that carbon has a faster recovery rate than glass, there is a significant difference in the effort required to cast consistently under tricky conditions, and at the end of a hard day's flyfishing a carbon rod will be the one that is more enjoyable to use.

The foregoing will apply to most small waters and those larger ones with some convenient bays, but what of the large stillwater with no appreciable bays or with considerable depths of water? Logically, it is possible to fish considerable depths only from a dam wall or a boat, most natural waters just do not have banks that shelve off to 20–30 ft (6–9 m) of water within casting distance. It is at such depths that the better fish may very well be caught with the use of a fast sinking line and a size 6 lure of the black or white variety, fished slowly across the bed of the lake. Sometimes a yellow fly may provoke a brown trout into taking, but this is certainly due to territorial instincts, and once one fish has been encountered, it is usual for others to follow.

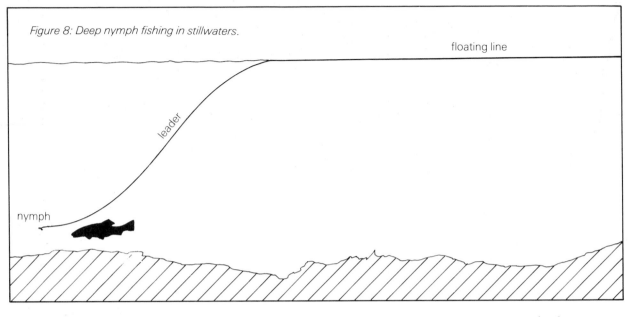

Figure 8: Deep nymph fishing in stillwaters.

floating line

leader

nymph

The most effective line for fishing the very deep water is a fast-sinking shooting taper. The light backing which enables a longer cast is dragged down quicker by the sinking line, and when retrieving the fly the backing also cuts through the water better and allows the line itself to 'hug' the bottom and therefore fish the fly more effectively.

The two major points to remember in early season fishing, after the very important slow retrieve, is that the takes from the trout will more than likely be cautious and should not be struck at, if at all, until a firm pull from the fish is felt. The other point concerns the choice of fly itself. In the early days, the fishing is sometimes quite active, with fish being caught regularly and takes missed, if the water has a healthy stock of fish. If the fishing has been good and it unaccountably quietens, a change of fly may well produce regular sport again. The reason for this must be that a fish hooked and lost, or pricked, when being presented with that same fly will be alarmed, and upon demonstrating its alarm will spread disquiet amongst the neighbouring fish.

SUMMER

Once the warmer weather has well and truly arrived, the fly fishing becomes infinitely more interesting and in general requires more thought and expertise. The main reasons for this are that the fish are on the move and looking for food, and many will become selective feeders. Also, many will have been in the fishery for some weeks, and having been pricked or alarmed in some way by fishermen, will become tackle shy. These fish are a worthwhile quarry because they will have

grown, if the water has the necessary food to support them, and will be in prime condition. To catch a fish that is wary to a degree is far more satisfying to the fisherman than to catch a stock fish that is new to the water and may snap at the first fly it sees in a bewildered attempt to feed itself in its alien environment.

During these summer days, the fishing becomes most interesting during the evening period, when there is an evening rise induced by a plentiful hatch of flies, usually buzzers or sedges on lakes and reservoirs. The fishing may be equally good and productive during the day, but bright sunshine and balmy days are definitely a disadvantage for trout fishing. Whereas rainbow trout are inclined to rove near the surface for their food during the day, bright sunshine will drive them deeper in the water and make it difficult to locate them. But by the same token, at some time during the heat of a summer's day it may be possible to scratch a worthwhile brown trout from the depths. During the day, the browns tend to retreat to deeper, and therefore cooler, water and will return to the shallows or the surface to patrol in search of food during the darker hours, being particularly active at dawn and dusk. As always, there are exceptions to every rule and so it often pays in trout fishing never to stick to what is correct in theory. The most successful trout fisherman is without question the one who is versatile.

Right When nymph fishing in poor light conditions, such as the early morning or late evening, great concentration is needed in order not to miss bites.

Nymph fishing

Fishing a nymph slowly across a gentle ripple with a floating line early in the morning or late in the evening can be most pleasurable, particularly when the hatch is matched correctly and the floating line regularly leaps out towards the centre of the fishery as some cruising trout has been deceived by the correctly presented artificial.

During summer there are many forms of fish food, and although the same nymphs may take trout all the season through, there is no doubt that at this time of the year some are more deadly than at other times. The Amber Nymph, an imitation of the sedge pupa, is a most successful fly, as is the Buzzer Nymph and Hare's Ear Nymph, to name just three of a very long list. Smaller hook sizes are normally essential and in order to fish these properly a lighter leader is an advantage, if not a necessity. The absolutely crucial deciding factor as to whether the fly will be taken or not could be the depth at which it is fished. The trout are set on a cruising depth as they search for food and often will not vary that depth by any amount at all, and so observation of the fish's behaviour in the water is essential.

If the nose and then the tail of the fish show above the surface (head and tailing), they will be taking something that is hatching just when it is at the surface. The occasional swirl at the surface indicates a fish deeper in the water taking a nymph as it ascends or even a corixa, snail or shrimp. The splashy, slurping rises mean that the fish is taking the insect dry, as it sits on the water.

A 9 ft 6 in (2.90 m) rod with a floating line fished from the bank on the occasions when fish are rising will provide as many fish as any other method. Quite often it will snare the biggest, though not usually as many large ones as lure fishing might.

Trout usually move up the wind in search of food. If a scum lane or calm lane passes near the bank, that is most likely to be the hot spot. During any sort of weather, fish will always be in such a feature.

The ideal position from the bank is fishing across the wind from a point. The fly, or team of flies, should be cast at right angles to the wind and either retrieved slowly or allowed to swing round in an arc, which very often produces many and confident takes. If the fish are right at the surface, some line flotant rubbed on the leader will keep the fly up in the water at eye level for the fish. It is a simple matter to de-grease the line with a compound, or mud as a last resort, if the fly is thought to be too high in the water.

If the fly is presented correctly and the fish are in a feeding mood, and providing as always that the correct fly is being used, the takes should register by the line drawing away, sometimes gradually, sometimes with a thump that takes you by surprise. Other times there will be just a tweak at the line nearest the fly, which you could miss very easily if your attention wanders ever so slightly. Total concentration is very important. Very many fly fishermen are broken at the leader by a fish which took so quickly that they were taken unawares. To hold the line tightly is to court disaster, but not to hold it tightly enough is equally likely to lead to frustration. The happy medium has to be found. Each take will have to be struck, lightly and firmly by raising the rod until the fish is felt, and then just a little bit more until the fish is held hard and the hook sinks in. The fight then begins.

Wet fly fishing

At certain times of the day, fishing a wet fly, an imitation of a hatched insect, may be the most effective way of taking trout.

It can be used in exactly the same way as fishing with nymphs, but for sheer enjoyment and excitement there is little that can better a team of wet flies fished loch-style in front of a drifting boat. There are a number of wet flies which prove particularly deadly, and although many improvements have been attempted over a long period of time, they have remained in their original form and carry on catching fish; a few variations also work well on their day.

A team of wet flies is usually employed, consisting of three or four flies with a flashy point fly, such as Dunkeld, Alexander, Mickey Finn or something which is sufficiently bright to attract a fish. The one or two droppers should be the imitative patterns such as Wickhams or Invicta (which both imitate sedges), Blae and Black, Greenwells Glory. The top dropper, or bob-fly, should be a heavily-dressed pattern, such as a Soldier Palmer, Sedge or even a small Muddler Minnow. The point of a heavily-dressed fly is that it will create a wake on the surface, and it should be held at the surface as long as the retrieve will allow, this will induce many fish to take which would otherwise have ignored the other flies. The flies should not be spaced too close together, and if the droppers are not the correct length, tangles may result during casting. As it is the individual's style which determines the length of the cast and number and length of droppers, only experience will provide the correct combination. It is vitally important, whatever the weather conditions, that neither the cast, nor the floating line leaves a surface wake. Although fish may still be caught if there is a wake, many will be deterred by it, and certainly only the most unwary of the better fish will fall to a clumsily presented and fished cast of flies.

Loch-style boat fishing entails casting to the front of a drifting boat, either freely drifting or slowed by a drogue, with a team of wet flies. The theory behind this method is that the fish will be moving up the wind, and the boat will be drifting to meet them. If the water is well stocked and the fish are inclined to feed at or near the surface, there should be plenty of action on a day which is warm and slightly overcast with a ripple or small wave on the water. Because of the mobility of loch-style fishing, people usually prefer to make short casts and retrieve by raising the rod before the flies are retrieved from the water and re-cast. The bob-fly should be fished so that it leaves a wake and at times the speed of retrieve may need to be faster than at others. In order to be able to fish the bob fly correctly a rod of at least 10 ft (3.05 m) in length is required and up to 11 ft 6 in or 12 ft (3.50 m or 3.65 m) would be ideal.

When the fish can be seen moving at the surface, a short line cast right on to their noses and retrieved immediately must be of interest to them. If it causes them to take fright, it will be obvious that something is wrong with the tackle or presentation. It is absolutely essential that the lowest profile possible is maintained in the boat as fish at close quarters will be easily frightened by a high silhouette long before they are within the short casting range which we are discussing. This in turn may lead the flyfisher to think that the fish are ignoring his tackle, so he constantly changes flies and becomes more frustrated. The fact is that the fish do not want to see his flies because they are aware of his presence. Attention to detail is critical.

If the fish are approaching the boat, or showing an interest in the flies and not taking them, it is often due to the flies being too large or perhaps just slightly the wrong colour, or not fished fast enough or slow enough. The first step is to change the fly at the point of the cast, changing the dropper should be the next step , and then the colour or pattern. The very largest fly that is necessary is a number 8 short shank, and success normally comes somewhere between that size and number 14. The fly may suddenly appear in the fish's field of vision, and due to the short cast, comes right to the surface and looks as though it may escape if the fish does not act quickly. This is a form of the induced take, and the takes are always swift as the fish turns hard on a quarry which he thinks may escape. The fight is usually energetic and thrilling as the fish thrashes on the surface or runs to the side or back of the boat, and it will require thoughtful playing.

A fish that is hooked at the surface will often thrash on the surface, or immediately launch itself into the air, or commence a series of underwater acrobatics, and the hookhold may not withstand this. In all instances the answer is to drop the point of the rod. Although all textbooks are correct in recommending that the rod tip is kept raised, there are certainly many exceptions to this rule. Keeping the point of the rod up serves to maintain a tight line to the fish, which is right, but what may be overlooked is that a tight line to a fish that has its head up will pull out the hook. The hook is also more likely to become loose or free if the fish continually twists and turns. In every instance, if the rod is pulled hard to one side, whilst maintaining pressure, the fish will stop the wild tactics and lower itself in the water; there are no exceptions, unless the hookhold fails.

The ideal places to find fish for loch-style wet fly fishing, or short-lining as it is also known, is drifting into or along a fairly shallow bank, or along the side of (not in) a wind lane or scum lane.

Lure fishing

During bright periods, and for the large part of those summer 'dog' days when the sky is clear and the light intense with hardly any wind to move the surface, the fish may be unwilling to show at or near the surface. It is then that they will have to be searched for, and lure fishing over deeper water can produce results.

Some fish, such as large brown trout, might well spend the greater part of their lives in deep water, making forays for nourishment only during the unsociable hours of twilight and darkness. These fish will take a properly presented lure, but other fish will be seeking the comfort of the cooling water near the bed of the lake and the darker depths.

If you are fishing from a bank where the bottom shelves off very steeply or from a boat anchored over deep water, the shooting head will be the more useful line by far for the task of deep fishing a lure. A rod of at least 9 ft 6 in (2.90 m) is ideal for bank or boat.

There are many types of lure, and a lure can be any colour in the rainbow and it will take fish at one time or another. This may be due to the fact that some colours fluoresce differently at depth. To give one example, white fluoresces into blue in the depths and white is a very effective colour for a lure. The most popular lures are either white or black based, usually with a dash of a bright colour such as yellow, green or red. Possibly the most effective lure is the Appetizer which has a white chenille body, white marabou underwing, squirrel tail over wing and throat and tail hackles of a mixture of red and green. Other very effective lures are the Sweeney Todd, Black Chenille, Black Ghost, Baby Doll, Perch Fry, Muddler Minnow (which must be the most versatile fly in the box in varying colours and sizes), and, of the predominantly orange lures, the Chief Needebah, Jersey Herd and Whiskey Fly.

Two handsome rainbow trout with the lures that caught them.

For fishing deep water, the boat should be anchored as firmly as possible, and whether bank or boat fishing the longer the cast the more effective it will be. Sometimes a fish will follow a lure some distance before eventually taking or refusing it. It is better to fish right on the bottom, retrieving slowly near features such as towers, sunken hedgerows, weed beds or humps on the lake bed. Fry, which form the major part of the large trout's diet, congregate near such features, and the object of a lure is to imitate these small fish, or to provoke aggression.

The retrieve of the lure should be slow, and the fish should not be struck until it is firmly felt. Often trout will tweak a lure several times during a retrieve before taking it, and to strike before it has taken firm hold would cause alarm to that fish and others in the area. As with all forms of flyfishing, it is vital that as little noise as possible, and preferably no noise, is made as that can warn the fish of the presence of its deadliest natural enemy. In particular, avoid wading. It disturbs both the fish, and the insects in the margins, and this discourages the fish from cruising near the edge.

Fishing the lure at depth is not the only effective way, nor is the slow retrieve the only answer. In fact, there never really is a complete answer, and trying something different from everyone else on the day could well achieve results.

A small lure, size 10 or 8, fished near the surface on a warm day can often be deadly for cruising rainbow trout, particularly if they are feeding on daphnia. Daphnia is sometimes called the water flea. It is a water insect about half the size of a pinhead and is present in most stillwaters. It collects together in vast numbers and is moved around by the water currents. It rises nearer the surface in darkness and sinks lower in bright light; the brighter the day, the lower will be the daphnia. It forms a large part of the rainbow trout's diet, particularly in the summer, and is often near the leeward bank. The trout swim through the clouds of daphnia, and a white lure fished slowly at the right depth will catch fish.

The surest way to catch fish from a moving boat is to cast the fly at right angles to the direction of drift and retrieve the fly slowly so that the fly follows round into an arc. As it passes the sharpest point of the curve it speeds up and the take will nearly always occur there, as the fly speeds up and changes direction at the same time. This is another variation of the induced take. You must determine the correct depth at which to fish but this can only be done by trial and error, interspersed with knowledge of the water, judgment and good fortune.

Dry fly fishing

When fish are taking a fly 'dry', they are feeding on an insect which is on the surface of the water, and is either recently hatched or hatching in the case of aquatic insects, or has returned to the surface of the water to lay its eggs and then died. Trout do not feed solely on aquatic insects, a large number of terrestrial insects become part of the diet in the summer months: drone flies, ladybirds and even ants and bees may have the misfortune to be blown onto the water, and these will be utilized to supplement the diet of any hungry trout in the vicinity.

The trout is attracted to a fly on the surface by the indentations that its body and legs make in the maniscus that can be seen easily from beneath the surface. If the insect struggles, the attraction appears to be all the more irresistible.

Dry fly fishing can provide a relaxing break during an otherwise strenuous day; and, rather than cease fishing, a dry fly may be watched over lunch. On the other hand, it can be taken much more seriously: attempting to match the hatch, stalking the cruising fish with care, and casting very precisely to intercept them.

Although the dry fly is floating on the surface or in the surface film, and depending on the food this distinction may be critical, the end of the leader at the fly should be submerged, even if only the first few inches, but the more leader that is sunk the better. A leader floating on the maniscus is a flashing danger sign pointing straight to the dry fly, and there will be no rises. The fly is usually sprayed with a flotant, or dipped into it, and dried by the false casting between casts, so that it will float on the next cast; the leader should be treated with a de-greasing compound or plain mud, which will make it sink.

The best rod is one that has plenty of through-action, of 8 ft to 9 ft (2.45 m to 2.75 m) in length; however, as far as accuracy is concerned, the action is more important than the length. For presentation of a dry fly, the ultimate line is a double taper floating AFTM 4, 5 or 6 and coupled with a light rod, the outfit should be a delight with which to fish; any fish caught will be a bonus. Accurate casting is all important because the fish being stalked are at or very near to the surface and cruising fairly slowly, and the fly is cast to a spot that will be in a fish's path. If the fly is in the wrong place, or presented clumsily, it is immediately rendered useless, unless it has, by sheer good fortune, pleasantly surprised a different trout.

The fly should be presented in the path of a rising fish and left to await results. The fly should not be moved after casting, as it will lose any appeal that it may have had. If the trout cruises past and ignores it, it should be retrieved and cast again, either to the same fish or a fresh target.

Trout all too often become very selective when taking dry insects, and unless the presented artificial approximates very closely indeed to the natural, it will be totally ignored. This occurs, for example, during the frequent hatches of Caenis, a tiny fly, too delicate to imitate, and so plentiful during its hatch that the artificial would only be picked out by a matter of luck anyway. These periods of total preoccupation by the trout are preceded, usually, by a short period when the fish become active and a few may be caught in a short space of time. The flyfisher, lulled into a sense of security, thinks that they are coming onto the feed at last. They are, but in the blink of an eye fish will be rising everywhere on the lake and no more will be taken, unless the odd one can be teased in some way. Sometimes at the end of the rise the odd one may take before retiring for the night.

During periods of preoccupation, it is essential that the flyfisherman maintains his observation and concentration on the water. If the object of the trout's attention is obvious and easily imitated, the correct imitation may produce results. If not, it must be back to the fly box and trial and error. As with all other flyfishing, the size and colour of the fly is important, but the height at which it rides on the surface may affect its attractiveness to the trout. Try out a variety of patterns to discover how interested the fish are. A bulge in the surface at the fly means that the trout has looked closely at the fly and rejected it. The same fish will not look at that fly again no matter how many times it is presented. The tackle and presentation should be examined, and perhaps a smaller fly tried, or one of a slightly different colour. Changing down in size is better than changing up when a fly has been refused; a larger fly works only when there is no hatch to speak of, so the fish are not preoccupied; or when they are preoccupied, and an imitation that is much larger than the natural may stand out to the degree that it appears more tempting. However, this seldom works, as the trout has an infuriating logic which escapes accurate interpretation.

There are a great many patterns of dry fly, as this form of flyfishing has been in existence longer than any other, but the main patterns that should be in every fly-box are Sedges, Olives, Black Gnat, Grey Duster, Tup's Indispensible, Coachman, White Moth and Mayfly, in sizes ranging from 18, or smaller in the case of some, up to an 8 or 10.

To cast accurately to a rising fish and have it take the fly with a swirl is the ultimate experience in flyfishing, but in dry-fly fishing the strike should not be immediate. If the fish still has its head up from the rise, a strike will pull the fly away from it. There should be a pause before the strike is made. Once the fish has its head down there is every chance that the hook will find a hold. Just how long the pause should be depends on a number of factors, the two main ones being: the length of the cast, which is affected by the tackle because a soft rod will not impart the strike to the fly as soon as a springy one would; and the speed of the fish when it takes, a casual rise needing a slightly longer pause than if the rise is of the slashing type. If a number of fish can be tempted to rise to the fly, and the strike can be timed to perfection, the day will be elating, and it is then easy to understand why some individuals become fanatical dry-fly enthusiasts.

AUTUMN

As the summer months draw to a close and autumn approaches, the flyfishing on stillwaters reaches its peak, for a number of reasons. The weather conditions become ideal, the balmy days of summer are replaced by cloudy, windy days which make the presentation of the fly that much easier. The water is still warm, but the fish, sensing the impending, comparatively barren days of winter, feed with urgency, taking full advantage of nature's larder, which is the legacy of the fruitful summer. These are the two main reasons why the trout that are caught at this time of the year may be better, on average, than throughout the rest of the season. Apart from the fact that they have been in the fishery longer and have grown, the larger fish are more reckless towards the end of summer and in the autumn.

The same principles apply to autumn trout fishing as to that in summer. The same patterns will produce results, but there are one or two methods which come into their own, due to the particular food available now, which was not previously in the water, or if it was there the fish were not paying it full attention.

Short-lining in front of a boat will still be as exciting as ever and nymph and dry-fly fishing from the bank or boat will be just as productive, but the method to beat all is dapping a daddy-long-legs (cranefly).

Dapping

For dapping, a longer rod than normally used in flyfishing is essential: at least 12 ft (3.65 m) and preferably 14 ft (4.25 m) is ideal. The technique is to hold the live or artificial daddy-long-legs in front of the boat so that it trips along the surface of the water, in the same way that the many insects blown off the land onto the water do. The rod is held high and the fly is carried forwards by the wind and held on the surface,

this would not be easy without a specially-made lightweight line, known as a blow line. This is a short line made up of many fibres, light in weight and bulky in diameter, which catches the wind and takes the fly that much further in front of the angler than it would ordinarily be. Dapping can be successful from the bank, but is at its most exciting from a boat. The fish produce electrifying takes in a number of forms: they may slash at the fly on the surface; or they may launch themselves from the water, taking the fly as they go or as they fall back. If the water is sensibly stocked and the fish have normal, healthy appetites, dapping the daddy-long-legs will produce a superb day's sport. The best conditions are overcast days, with a ripple or wave on the surface. Naturally this form of fishing is best when the insects are being blown onto the water, but after the daddy-long-legs have dissappeared the fish may still be willing to come to the dapping method.

Surface lures

Because of the trout's nomadic tendency, especially the rainbow, at this time of the year, a small lure fished on a floating line, either at or very near the surface can entice the fish, who will move some distance to take the lure. The most effective lures will be those that have a marabou wing, as the action of this material seems to have a much greater attraction than some of the more rigid materials. Hair wings can also be very effective.

Of the surface lures that catch fish during the autumn, the most popular is the Muddler Minnow in its various forms and colours. It is fished either on its own, in larger sizes, or as a bob-fly with a team of flies. As a bob-fly, it should be around size 10, or 12 at the most, and be trimmed rather more neatly than it would otherwise be, because the aerodynamics of a bulky fly affect the final delivery of the cast and will induce tangles. This becomes very frustrating when fish are rising all around, but the biggest disadvantage of a tangle is that the resulting knot may go unnoticed and a fish may be lost because of the weakened leader; and regardless of what the cynics say, it is always the big one that gets away.

Fishing a Muddler Minnow on its own on a floating line, or with a small lure as the dropper, the fly can be much larger and bulkier. Indeed, this is preferable; the rounder the head, the more it disturbs the surface, making it more visible to the fish. It should be cast downwind and pulled back in long strips. The wake it leaves and the 'pops' on the surface will mark its presence, and often the fish may follow for some distance. The excitement of seeing a bow-wave following the fly can be too much, but the fly should be retrieved at the same speed; to vary the retrieve always puts off the fish. At the take, the retrieve should be continued until the fish is felt. Trout often roll over on the fly without taking it, but will then take it from beneath within a very short time, and if you strike before the fish has taken, you will lose it. Anglers have their own rules for Muddler Minnow fishing and dealing with the many follows it induces. Some say, look the other way and ignore what is happening; others say, take the fly off the water and lay it back in the same place. I have never found either to be more successful but, there again, if there is a fish behind my fly, I can never ignore it and would only deprive it of the fly under extreme circumstances. On one particular late-September day, I recall fishing from a boat at Draycote with a Muddler Minnow and early in the day a brown trout in the 3 lb (1.35 kg) class launched itself into the air, about 1 yd (1 m) behind my fly, turned in the air in particularly nonchalant fashion, and re-entered the water nose first. This was puzzling behaviour until, about three seconds later, a vicious take almost tore the line from my grasp, and after a hectic fight from a brutish brown trout, I netted a fish which looked to be the same one, but having not encountered this before I was not certain. However, the same thing happened a number of times during the day and every time a fish cleared the water near the fly, a really hard take followed shortly, but there was never any sign of the fish before or after it cleared the water. Another point about that day was that the fish came in a comparatively very small area of what appeared to be open water at the mouth of a large bay. It became possible to predict where the takes would start and when they would cease due to the precision of their location. I finished with a limit of fish by early evening, averaging 3 lb (1.35 kg) in weight, most of them browns. The method can be exasperating but it can also be exhilarating. The only rules to follow are: never persevere with it if no results are forthcoming within a short space of time, if the fish are inclined to take a Muddler they will soon show it; and make sure that there is a wave on the water and that the sky is overcast. The fish will very seldom take a Muddler at the surface on a sunny day with flat calm. If it is tried on a flat calm surface, in a desperate attempt to induce some action, it must be fished very slowly, and is at its best over about 8 ft (2.5 m) of water. The results are never consistent when conditions are not ideal.

Fishing the margins

During the height of the summer months, the fish may tend to desert the margins if the water is still and the sun high, the shallows being uncomfortable for them. However, as the water cools during autumn, they will

A trout is hooked, played and netted successfully on this put-and-take fishery.

return to these shallows, particularly because coarse fish fry will be amongst the weed beds, and because the increasing winds oxygenate the water.

The weeded margins of all stillwaters during autumn become the haunts of the fry-feeding trout, and it is from these areas that the larger trout are often caught by lure fishing methods. The area will be particularly attractive to larger trout if there is deep water nearby. The trout give themselves away by hurtling into the shoals of fry and turning amongst them, snapping and thrashing with their tails. It may be that some injured fry will be left stunned, and the trout will return to mop them up at a more leisurely pace.

Such flies as Appetizer and Perch Fry lures will attract trout now, but many patterns imitative or reminiscent of small fry will be successful; the deciding factor is the speed of the retrieve. Because shallow water is being fished, a slow-sinking line or floating line is ideal because the rate of retrieve must be slow. In some instances it pays to leave the fly static. It must be remembered that the fish are not in the margins constantly. Once a trout has established a feeding area when it is taking fry, it will not stray from that area, and will hit the fry again and again. The fly must be kept in the water as long as possible to stand a chance of being on the fish's nose on one of its feeding forays. Some lures are designed to float, and are fry-shaped so that from below they may appear to be one of the stunned small fry mentioned earlier. The occasional twitch of the lure may provoke explosive action from the trout. Early morning and late evening are the most productive periods for fry-feeding fish. This is probably because of the proximity of the flyfisher to the water. During the brighter parts of the day any fish that are still feeding may detect the human presence. It is also true that the trout are more active when the light is not strong. Wherever possible, the fly should be retrieved along the weed-beds and not at right angles to the water's edge; in so doing, the fly will be visible to the fish more easily and for longer.

WINTER

Once the productive summer and autumn months have elapsed the trout return to their dour moods of the spring and will only infrequently sport on particularly warm days. They also lose condition quickly due to breeding tendencies, and it is not sporting to catch out-of-condition fish.

It is for these reasons that the majority of stillwaters close their gates to anglers during the colder months. Most fisheries close at the end of October or November. Because the rainbow trout has been introduced into these islands and does not breed naturally, except in a very few isolated instances, it is arguably not subject to the same close season rights as our native brown trout. Therefore, small fisheries find a way round the close season by stocking only rainbow or hybrid trout. In any event, these fish also lose condition and to date, despite exhaustive cross-breeding, no breeder has managed to hybridize trout that will stay in condition all year round at a sensible cost.

Because of breeding tendencies, the fish will congregate round any flowing water if they are going through the motions of spawning or cleaning themselves on gravel. These are obviously the fish to be avoided. The better fish, still with some firm flesh and silver scales, will be in deeper water and will take a fly fished slowly in exactly the same way as it would be in the spring. The same patterns will apply: Pheasant Tail Nymph, Black Lure, Appetizer, White Lure, Black Ghost, and so on. Deep and slow are the points to bear in mind whether fishing lure or nymph.

Trout fishing on rivers

INTRODUCTION

Although fishing for trout in rivers and streams may appear to be vastly different from fishing stillwaters, the quarry behaves in very much the same way in all environments, and it is only the techniques which require adaptation. It is difficult to recommend river and stream fishing as opposed to stillwater fishing, or vice versa. For my own part I commenced flyfishing on stillwaters, and then took a rod on a chalk stream for a number of years whilst continuing to fish reservoirs and lakes. I do not currently hold a rod on any stream due to the pressure of commercialism, which induced an artificial situation on the water. In any event, I would not have missed my regular dawn visits to the Kennet for anything, and I learnt almost everything I know about the fish's reaction to lines, flies, footfalls, and so on, by observing the fish in the clear water of that chalk stream. I also learnt much about the feeding habits, and habits in general, of brown and rainbow trout and because of the exquisiteness of fishing for trout in running water, I would recommend any flyfisherman to do likewise; there is much enjoyment and sport to be experienced.

The larger rivers of the United Kingdom can be fished quite adequately with a light reservoir outfit such as a 9 ft 6 in (2.90 m) rod and an AFTM 6 or 7 line. A longer rod may be necessary on rivers where a lengthy cast is required to cover rising fish. Having said that, there are definite problems encountered on almost all rivers where a long cast is made, and it boils down to the presentation of the fly to the fish. As this is the criteria in all flyfishing, I may seem to be stating the obvious. However, the would-be river flyfisherman has far more to contend with than his stillwater counterpart in the presentation of the fly.

When a long cast is made on any running water (except those with a very long and very wide glide), the floating line, which is cast so that it crosses the current, will at some time during its journey downstream be pulled or pushed by a different current from that carrying the fly, causing the fly to behave in an unnatural manner. Sometimes this is attractive to the fish, but in many instances they will become suspicious to the point of fleeing the vicinity. Always remember that the fly must travel on the water at the rate and in the manner in which the trout is accustomed to seeing all its food arrive. The fact is that trout in running water, once established, do not wander far and will leave a feeding station only when alarmed or seeking cover for another reason, such as shade. It is essential, therefore, that when fishing with the fly in running water, the fisherman has an eye not only on his quarry but also on the various currents that are present and which may affect the presentation of the fly, particularly the dry fly.

In the chalk streams and small rivers, drag on the fly is easier to combat and it is great fun to fish these waters with a traditional rod. On small waters where there is vegetation hampering casting and overhanging trees, a 6 ft (1.85 m) Farlow's Midge, a split cane rod, is perfect. With the correct line it is still possible to achieve an appreciable distance if a long cast is needed, but a rod that is any shorter than 7 ft 6 in (2.30 m) in split cane needs to have a firm action. The ideal lines for fishing running water are floating forward tapers and AFTM 5 or 6, but if delicacy is the prime consideration, a double taper cannot be bettered.

The beauty of fishing streams and rivers is so enthralling that many flyfishermen become totally absorbed in it and spend a great deal of money on their tackle. This is nice but not necessary, particularly in the case of the reel, which is simply a device to store or hold line. There are many types of small river and stream reels on the market at costs which vary considerably, but a reservoir reel will be adequate at a push.

The aspiring stream fisherman can walk into a tackle shop and spend a great deal of money, or he can make do with what tackle he may possess for fishing stillwaters. There is a happy medium in that the tackle need not cost the earth, and it is certainly preferable to

When wading is necessary, it should be done with extreme care to avoid a slip or fall. It is also essential that you do not frighten away any fish in the area.

own a stream-fishing outfit. There are companies of rod-makers offering split cane at very reasonable prices, and the sweetness of a light split cane rod and the lively feel it has when playing a fish cannot be beaten. There are various types of man-made materials on the market, glass fibre, carbon fibre, boron, and compounds which incorporate some of these, and the price range from bottom to top is vast.

In the case of the reel, again there are exotic productions of carbon fibre, magnesium, and so on, but a single action fly reel from one of the well-known manufacturers will serve the beginner well. I still own a perfectly serviceable Intrepid Regular from my early flyfishing days and this type of reel is inexpensive and easily repaired if any problems arise. Having said that, I also own several more expensive reels which are a delight to fit to the rod. The price must be dictated by the individual and his requirements.

The other essential items, apart from obvious necessities such as priest, flies, and leader, are a light shoulder bag (game bag) which holds all tackle and still allows mobility, and a folding landing net. The type of landing net which clips to the bag and which unfolds with a flick of the wrist is ideal. In stream fishing, the best results are obtained by roving the bank and stalking the fish, even when they cannot be seen.

The cost of stream fishing in the United Kingdom can be very reasonable, or prohibitive. It is necessary to ensure before fishing a stream or river for the first time that one is fully conversant with the rules laid down by the owner or the controller of the water. For instance, on the highland and moorland streams and rivers virtually any method of fly fishing, upstream and downstream, may be allowed, whilst on hallowed waters such as the Rivers Test and Itchen dry-fly-only is usually the rule and in addition the hatch must be matched.

It is usually possible, like finding the right tackle, to find a water which is a happy medium. The moorland and highland rivers produce superb sport in the form of small wild brown trout, which by comparison with reservoir trout or regular stock fish may be regarded as puny, but they are an invigorating challenge to all stream fishermen and there is always the chance of a better fish coming along. Although the average size of fish in wild waters may be small, if you use the correct tackle sport can be plentiful. It may also be rather more difficult to catch the small fish of these waters than it would be to tempt the wallowing, overfed and recently-stocked trout of some rivers that are represented as holding wild fish and which command an inordinately high fee for a season or daily rod. The fish which live in river and stream have advantages that

their stillwater counterparts are unable to claim: they have an uneven, and sometimes snag-ridden habitat and they have the current, which lends assistance to an already powerful fish. The fact that the trout lives in running water and therefore needs to fight the current constantly to lie in one position means that it can be more powerful for its weight than a lake fish might be, and it can provide an unexpectedly fierce battle.

The depth at which the flyfisherman must fish is as important as it would be fishing stillwaters. In any running water holding a head of trout it would be most unusual to find a deep pool that did not hold a number of fish living near the bottom, and beds of streamer weed often hide trout that will boldly dart from cover to take food and then dart back. Trees that hang close to the water will hide trout residing there for the food that falls from the branches, for the shade provided, and because they are safe from all natural enemies. The presence of these latter trout is often given away by the gallery of anglers' flies adorning the branches hanging to the water, and these are the fish that provide the greatest challenge. To cast a fly beneath an overhanging tree, or upstream so that it floats beneath the tree and then to have it taken is the ultimate experience in stream fishing.

In general, you need only a floating line for stream fishing because the fish are more inclined to move for what they consider to be edible. A fish lying in deep water will rise to the surface for a dry fly, and if it is necessary to fish deeper a leaded nymph will usually provide the answer. Because it is not always possible to maintain constant contact with the fly, it is necessary to be able to see what is happening to the fly if it sinks, and this is done by watching the line. It would not be either practicable or necessary to fish a dry fly with a sinking line.

When fishing on streams or rivers, you will often encounter other flyfishermen who have taken up a position because of a particular fish that is presenting a challenge. The correct procedure is to pass the angler, giving him a wide berth unless invited to do otherwise, and leave him to his fish, bearing in mind that a shadow on the water or a careless footfall on the bank may ruin his patient efforts thus far.

Wading should be avoided if at all possible. Apart from the obvious danger of frightening fish from the immediate vicinity, there is also the damage it causes to the insect life in the water. Having said this, some rivers are not effectively fished without wading, but it should be done with care for safety reasons. Also, it would be most improper to wade uninvited within a reasonable distance of another fisherman, whether he is wading or not.

Playing the fish in running water

As mentioned previously, trout (and grayling) in running water have the advantage over stillwater trout, in that they are invariably aided by the current, and usually by obstacles such as tree roots, weed-beds and floating obstacles as well. The fish, if it has been resident in the area for more than a brief period, will be perfectly familiar with its surroundings and upon feeling the hook will instantly bolt for cover, often in a downstream direction.

It is disadvantageous to the flyfisher to play a fish from upstream because the weight of the fish is increased by the drag of the current. Also, the fish is pointing straight up the line, which means that if the hook-hold is even slightly suspect, there is more chance of it pulling free. If, when trying to pull the fish upstream, it gains the security of a weed-bed or snag, the direction of the pull must immediately be transferred to downstream.

Some trout, upon feeling the hook, will bolt through a weed-bed and emerge the other side. The fish must be given slack, and the pull then exerted again gradually, in the hope that the fish may be gently led back through the weeds while remaining hooked. The current aids the angler, by applying pressure on the fish through the drag on the line, therefore some slack line can be given. Just how much pressure depends on the speed of the current and the amount of line on the water.

Once the fish has been brought into open water, it is preferable to gain a downstream position from it, and once it has been played out, its head can be lifted and the current can be used to carry it into the waiting net. Once netted it should be either unhooked and returned, or despatched before it is unhooked, depending upon its destiny. In both cases, the fish should be out of the water for only the shortest possible time. If a fish is to be returned to the water, it is best played out as quickly as possible so that it will have some reserves of energy to allow it a speedy recovery. When handling the fish, it is best done in the net, which will provide some grip and make sure that it is not handled with dry hands. Of course it is better not to handle a fish to be returned at all. It is possible to bring it to the bank, grip the fly with finger and thumb and then the fish is likely to shake itself free, whereupon it can race back to freedom and further growth to provide sport for the future.

SPRING

Most stream fishing that is controlled or owned begins in late spring, around early to mid-April, but the wild waters of moorland and highland usually start on 1st March, which often arrives amid snow storms, when the water is particularly cold and only the bravest and most dedicated of flyfishermen venture into the bleak countryside in search of the small brown trout which still provide willing sport. It is possible to locate a surprising amount of stream fishing at this time of the year, and one is always assured of finding seclusion. The rivers which hold wild trout are usually in spate at this time of year, and locating the fish can be very difficult, but in the streams the level stays fishable and sufficiently clear for the fishing to be consistent.

Surprisingly, early in March, brown trout will readily come to a dry fly, but never a large one; a small pattern such as a Black Gnat, Tup's Indispensible, Grey Duster or Alder Fly may work very well but it is desirable to have clear, or reasonably clear water conditions. Although the fish will take a fly in cold water, if the water temperature has recently been reduced, due to melting snow or heavy rainfall, the fish will almost certainly be inclined not to feed until the temperature has stabilized.

Because it is not practicable to fish a dry fly from an upstream position, the stalking of the trout should be commenced at the downstream limit of the beat to be fished, and the fly cast upstream, with an upstream change of position after each possible area of water has been covered. It is quite likely that no fish will be seen rising, and any fish induced to rise to the fly will appear out of the blue, but every likely piece of water should be carefully fished over until the angler is satisfied that there is either nothing there, or that what fish are there will not be induced to rise. If fish are there, they will usually show an interest in one fly or another, and once a fly has interested them, the same fly repeatedly cast over them may well produce a rise eventually. This could be because a properly presented dry fly cast repeatedly over the same fish may eventually persuade it that a hatch has started, and that it should be taking full advantage of it at this time of the year when food may be scarce. On the other hand, it might be that the trout will only take a fly that is presented over precisely the point at which food will be taken. Both of these theories have been put to the test on many occasions, and both have been proved. On one occasion a trout showed more and more interest in a fly which was being cast within striking distance, and became more and more agitated, until it finally took the fly when it came close enough. On other occasions, trout have been seen to rise in one precise position, and all other flies, including artificials, were ignored unless they passed that exact spot. This is more than likely where a current is channelled through trailing weeds, or diverted by a rock. By

Pools such as this one, on a moorland stream, can contain lively fish early in the season.

precision casting and delicate presentation, such a fish will take the fly readily when it is at the chosen spot. Usually such fish are relatively easy to deceive because they see the fly riding down on the fast current only briefly before it reaches the taking point and they will dart up to take it and do not inspect it as a fish in slower waters would have time to do.

On the riparian-owned or carefully controlled chalk streams, it is normal for dry-fly fishing only to be allowed in springtime, if not for the entire season, whilst on the moorland and highland streams it is possible to fish dry, wet or nymph throughout. Although dry fly fishing is very entertaining and usually productive it is quite possible that the most successful method will be the downstream wet fly. For this, fishing is commenced at the top or upstream end of the beat and the flies are fished methodically downstream. Theoretically it is possible to cover the water more thoroughly with wet flies, although the flies will not actually fish much deeper than a dry fly would. A team of flies numbering three or four are normally em-

ployed, and they are, of necessity, small flies and will usually be more effective if they are sombre in colour. Some very productive patterns are dressed 'spider'-style. That is, they are flies that do not have an actual wing, but a single hackle lightly wound immediately behind the eye of the hook. These are used to great effect particularly in Scotland and Ireland throughout the year. Because these flies are sunk, they are not subject to the same careful methods as dry fly. Anything which is below the surface and is actually in the water may reasonably be expected to make an attempt to escape not only from a watery grave but also from the hungry clutches of the trout. It is for this reason that trout are never so wary of a wet fly which is moved against the current.

The normal way to fish the downstream wet fly is to cast at a slightly downstream angle across the current and allow the flies to swing around with the current. Although presentation is arguably easier or not so important, it is imperative that the flies sink and do not skate across the surface as they swing across; they will certainly not be acceptable to the trout if they do so. If a different current is causing this effect, the answer is to mend the line upstream and use the rod tip to manipulate the line in order to give the flies the necessary time to sink before they start their swing across the current. Of course a sinking line may be employed, but is only practicable if the water to be fished is particularly deep and preferably slow moving. In any other water a sinking line would snag any obstruction in the water on its downstream journey. In fact it is surprising just what effects the currents can produce. In fast water, a fly which is sunk will very often be pushed further below the surface by a fast current, and in a pool that appears to be full of deep and fast water, the water will be fast near the surface only. Beneath the fast water the current is negligible and the trout live in peace and tranquility, feeding on the food which is pushed down to them by the eddy caused by the conflicting currents. If trout are known or suspected to be holding in a pool which is deep, they will be unlikely to rise when the water is cold, and the best way to reach them is by casting upstream and allowing the flies to tumble through the water to them as their food usually does.

To return to the downstream wet fly, the rod tip must be used to manoeuvre the line effectively so that the flies do not skate, but it must also be used to try to hold the flies in a position which will be likely to produce a take from the trout. Such likely places are where fast water meets slower water or where the current swings around a bend. The flies should be held as long as possible in such positions with only the minimum of movement, and then the rod tip used to work the flies until they are immediately downstream, when they can be retrieved against the current without actually passing through the vision of the trout. The takes from wild trout often come as the flies are held in the current 'on the dangle', and can be particularly difficult to connect with due to the speed with which they occur. Total concentration is required. If nothing is forthcoming from one cast the next one should be made from one step further downstream. In this way the flies cover the water in an arc which is continually moving downstream, and the water is covered thoroughly.

Experience gained from fishing the same water on numerous occasions will provide ideas about where the most likely lies are for trout in any particular river, and which are the best fly patterns to use. It is amazing how different one river can be from another, and when fishing a completely new water there is no substitute for local knowledge.

On the chalk streams and stocked rivers throughout England, the fishing is more expensive and the trout perhaps more plentiful, and larger due to stocking policies. The banks are mown and the water is generally slower moving and interesting in a different way from the rough rivers and streams. Day tickets may be bought on some rivers, although they are so sought after by enthusiasts that they command a high price for a one-day per week rod throughout the season. As with the rough waters, small dry flies will be of more interest to the trout than a large one and similar patterns to the rough water ones will succeed. The difference in the chalk streams is the fact that they are clear, when weather conditions are right, and the fish are visible early in the year due to the lack of weed growth.

Etiquette is strict on chalk streams, and all fishing should be upstream. This means that the flyfisherman is at all times downstream of the fish being cast to. It also means that anglers will not interfere with one another's fish and fishing. Movements should be stealthy because the banks of these waters are soft and transmit vibrations easily through the water to the fish.

Having successfully stalked a fish to within casting range, the next stage in upstream dry fly should be to take in the surroundings; for example, is there any foliage that will interfere with the back-cast, and are any trees overhanging the water, which may impede the passage of the fly to the correct position. The speed and direction of the current will have to be taken into consideration, as will the distance upstream that the fly will have to be cast to cover the fish properly. Generally speaking, a fish that is lying in deeper water will need more time, but deep water tends to be slower than shallow water, so the length of the cast above the fish will be about right in many cases. As a rule-of-thumb, the cast to the fish should be at, say, 45° to the bank, unless impeded by vegetation or the current is tricky. If the fish is close to the near bank it is essential to make the angle of the cast steeper.

It is usually easy to tell if a fish that is lying in open water is taking, by observing him for a short time. When satisfied that the fish is worth casting to and that there are no great problems, sufficient line should be stripped from the reel to allow the fly to reach the required position upstream and then it should be cast with the minimum of false-casts. The business of stripping line from the reel progressively as the false-casts are made looks very impressive, perhaps, but it frightens many fish. To have a fly-line zipping through the air at high speed directly over or near a fish time and time again will certainly put the fish down. It must also be remembered that there may be other fish in the vicinity that have gone unnoticed and if they become alarmed and bolt for cover, they will certainly take the intended quarry with them as they pass. If the fish is covered successfully, that is, correctly, a number of times but shows no interest, different flies should be tried, if it still refuses it should be left. If it shows interest but refuses the fly, it should be tried again with the same fly for only a few casts and then the fly

When fishing clear, low water, take cover behind bankside vegetation. If there is none, you can keep a low profile by kneeling.

The wild brown trout of highland and moorland rivers are relatively small in size but they fight hard and provide exciting sport.

changed for something similar or smaller, or both. When the fish eventually takes a dry fly, it has its head in an upward-tilted position; if the strike is made too soon the hook will simply skid through the bony part of the fish's mouth and come free. The fish must be given time to turn back down with the fly before the strike, and the hook should pull into the scissors or take a firm hold elsewhere in the mouth.

If contradictory currents exist in the casting area and are causing the fly to drag, the fly will be ignored and may put the fish down, the answer is to cast a line with sufficient slack to eliminate the drag. This can be done after the cast has been made, but is not really satisfactory because it causes surface disturbance over and above the actual cast. It is better to cast slightly overlength, and to pull the fly back slightly before the line hits the water, this causes the line to snake and will create some slack; only the actual cast will tell if it is enough. Another way of creating slack line to avoid drag is to cast overlength, and on the final delivery, cast the fly just to the required point and drop the rod tip as low as possible. As the fly travels downstream, line must be recovered, but it is unwise to maintain

tight contact with the fly because this will create drag: just enough to allow the line to be tightened by the raising of the rod tip, is perfect. Once the fish has been covered and the fly is downstream of him it can be picked off the water and re-cast to cover him again, preferably with a single false cast because the correct length will by now have been found.

SUMMER

With the arrival of the warm weather, many changes occur to heighten the flyfishing in rivers and streams. Some of these changes are obvious, but others may not be so. Obviously the most important change, and the one which brings about all others, is the increase in water temperature. This in turn promotes the growth of weed in the river, and insects propagate freely. Others that have lain dormant in or on the bed of the stream will carry on with their life cycle, and the fish will take full advantage of all these facts. Trout will move from deep water into shallow runs and will take up feeding positions in stronger currents than they would be willing to do in cooler water, the reason for this being that the energy expended in remaining in faster water can be easily replenished by the abundance of available food.

During this summer period the fish will continue to

This stretch of the Itchen has much about it to attract fish. The trees and bankside vegetation provide plenty of shade and shelter, and a steady flow ensures a good supply of food.

Even in summer a strong wind can make accurate casting difficult.

feed in the same way that they did in the spring, but the pace will be 'stepped up'. They will be more willing to move some distance to take a fly and will invariably have an eye cocked to the surface. Whereas in the cooler weather trout will lie in one position and rarely move far to take food, in the summer a feeding fish will be seen to dart from one position to another as it takes food, almost as though quartering the river bed. The distance it moves up or down stream will remain fairly constant and these fish will only move further in an up or down stream direction if they are startled. Provided that it is not alarmed by clumsy casting, a single fish may provide a fair time of interesting flyfishing.

It is at the start of the summer period that the most exciting event in the flyfishing calendar occurs–the mayfly hatch. The mayfly is a large insect which, in the nymph stage, lives in the gravel of clean rivers and streams for two years. When the temperature of the water is sufficiently high, they ascend to the surface and, carried swirling by the current like elegant sailing vessels, they emerge as a grown insect and take off into the air. Sometimes they are few in numbers, but often they form large clouds, dancing up and down. They mate, and the females return to the water to lay their eggs, sitting on the surface momentarily to eject a number of eggs at a time until all the eggs have been laid. Whereupon they lie on the surface of the water as spent flies, at the mercy of the many trout which take advantage of this prolific and succulent insect. The whole cycle from nymph to spent mayfly takes twenty-four hours, and then the cycle for the egg begins again. This event usually takes place from mid-May to mid-June, and on most waters lasts for two weeks. As mayflies are large insects, over 1 in (2.5 cm) long in most cases, the trout will be feeding avidly upon them at all stages, as they emerge from their shucks into adult life, as they lay their eggs and as they return to the water fully spent. It is important to observe a fish taking mayfly regularly to see just what the fish is actually taking. It may be that it is taking a hatching nymph or spent fly, or in some cases they will take only the shucks, which are empty. I once spent some time covering a very nice brown trout which would not look at my fly, and yet he was taking mayfly regularly as they passed over him. Seeking respite from the frustration of trying to tempt it with a number of mayfly patterns, I sat and watched and saw that it was taking the mayfly in one small area of water, smaller in size than a pocket handkerchief, which was preceded by a trailing willow branch behind which it firmly stayed. This in itself did not present an impossible problem, but the interesting point was that it was ignoring the fully spent mayfly and taking those that still had some life in them, those that vibrated the

meniscus with their wings in their final dying moments. Returning to a fishing position, I continued to cast and the first time that I passed an imitation over the taking position, I twitched the rod tip, which moved the fly. This resulted in the fish smashing my imitation, which it had ignored previously. I was fast into a very respectable brown trout which would normally have fled a long way if the fly presented to it had been unnaturally moved in any way. Fish will become preoccupied with mayfly in one form or another, and they sometimes become oblivious to everything else around them. This is not to say that they will be caught more easily; it is simply that the choice of targets for the flyfisherman is more abundant, and sometimes it is necessary to choose with care which fish to cover, to make sure that the best limit bag available is taken. The best time for the rise to the mayfly is early morning and evening. The fish rise confidently, splashing and slashing at the surface repeatedly. The stomachs of the trout become distended with mayfly and yet they continue to feed.

In those waters where mayfly are particularly abundant, the surface in the evening will become littered with spent mayfly, and trout may be difficult to tempt due to the fact that they are spoilt for choice. I have found that one particular pattern, based on a traditional one, works exceedingly well. Dressed on a long-shank size 10 hook (fine wire), three cock pheasant tail fibres form the tail (separated); the body is black gossamer silk, with a palmered badger hackle from eye to bend, and ribbed with oval tinsel; the main hackle is natural guineafowl spun behind the eye twice; and the whole fly is tied in with black tying silk. This represents a dark mayfly (there are numerous species), and is slightly on the large side. It also has to be liberally treated with flotant, otherwise it sinks and in any event it floats very low in the water, which is probably the secret of its success. Whilst all mayflies barely bend the meniscus as they float by, this pattern severely dents it and is therefore immediately more noticeable to the fish. I find in general that mayfly patterns with wings tied as spun hackles are more successful than those tied with upright wings. However, as I tend to use these patterns more, I am bound to be more successful with them. This is the chicken-and-egg situation, which is common in flyfishing. Many flyfishers find confidence in a particular pattern and will use that almost to the exclusion of others, and then profess it to be the best pattern on that water. It is as well to treat advice with caution; when recommending a pattern to be the best on the water, the angler offering advice may tie his flies with a slight difference from another or from a shop-bought pattern, and the fish find that version alone particularly interesting. This is more important on rivers and streams, but does also apply to stillwater flies.

Although wet fly and nymph (where allowed) tactics still catch fish, the summer period is most enjoyable for the fact that there are always fish rising in some part of the river, for a short period of time after the end of the mayfly hatch, the trout may become quiet and less inclined to rise, but things soon return to normal and they will again rise to the usual insects, which are still on the water but to some degree have been ignored in favour of the mayfly.

The rises will occur most frequently in early morning and later in the day as the sun loses its heat and intensity, but there is always the odd fish rising to provide a sporting chance of being able to cover something throughout the day. The flies which will be in evidence throughout the summer are other Ephemerids such as the olives, sedges and many land-borne insects. The fish which rise throughout the day will be less particular than those which rise in the evening. The evening fish have been induced to rise by an abundance of a particular species of fly and will not normally deviate from that species, except for the odd fish. It is then very important to match the hatch, and this can be done by simple observation of the insects on the surface, and what is seen to be taken by the trout. The patterns which are most useful in the fly-box through the summer will be various mayfly patterns, of course, various olive patterns, various sedge patterns, Tup's Indispensible, Iron Blues, Ginger Quill and a range of others which can be selected by browsing through shops and fly-tying books and guides. Another useful place to gain knowledge of the flies taking fish on a particular water is the record book that is often somewhere on the beat. Each pattern should be available in sizes ranging from small to fairly large (large in some patterns is much smaller than large in others).

The fish will be more widely dispersed through the river or stream, perhaps due to heavier stocking where stocking takes place; but resident fish will have moved from spring lies to areas which will provide a regular supply of food. As usual, there will always be fish in the deep, slow-moving pools, but other fish will be seen feeding over patches of gravel or clear river bed. It appears that trout prefer to feed over open patches of river bed, but it is probable that these fish are more easily seen. There must be just as many which blend in with weed and have to be sought more carefully. Trout will also hide beneath streamer weed, which grows anywhere. This weed usually separates at some point, and a fly passed along the 'corridor' thus formed stands a very good chance of being taken by a fish that may be taking refuge underneath.

Altogether, the summer is a particularly enjoyable time for the dry-fly fisherman and there may be no need whatsoever to try any other method because there will always be a trout in the river that is willing to rise, and almost all of the trout will at some period rise to a dry fly, natural or artificial. As with all dry-fly fishing, it is important that the first few inches of the leader are sunk, but the most important part is to avoid drag on the fly.

To wander the rivers and streams in the clear comfortable air of summer, whether the rocky banks of rough waters or the hallowed green of the chalk streams, with a light rod, and to be able to cast a dry fly to a rising fish, or a likely position, and to be able to induce that fish to take is an experience that completes every flyfisher's education and one that will be enjoyed and relived time and time again.

AUTUMN

As the year progresses into autumn, the sun loses much of its power, and the fly hatches become shorter and then non-existent except on the warmest of days. The trout then turns its attention mainly to sub-surface food in the form of shrimps, and bottom-crawling nymphs such as caddis larvae, corixae and so on. There will still be rising trout, but the majority will be looking for food under the surface and it is now that fishing the nymph will become most productive. Most fisheries allow the upstream nymph to be fished from July onwards and rough streams are open to the method all the season, but autumn is the time when it becomes most useful on the chalk streams. Upstream nymph means that the fly should be fished from a downstream position by casting the fly upstream. In any event, this is the best possible way to fish a nymph because it means that the slack line thus given allows the nymph to sink deeper and therefore fish at the level at which the trout are feeding.

The water will have started to cool, but the trout will still be in swift water as much as they were in the summer, and will occupy much the same lies until the water really cools down. For nymph fishing the most successful patterns will undoubtedly be variations of the Pheasant Tail Nymph, weighted and unweighted, shrimp patterns in different colours, corixa patterns, 'shell-back'-type nymphs and nymphs tied in the same style as the Pheasant Tail but with various materials in different colours. Straightforward patterns, such as Stickflies and Black and Peacock Spider should also be included in the selection of the nymph-fisher. It seems that the most successful nymphs incorporate seal fur somewhere in the pattern, or are almost entirely tied with seal fur.

The fisherman crouches to keep a low profile on the river bank as he casts to a trout he has seen feeding under the willows.

Apart from the obvious differences between nymph and dry fly, there are some vital differences in approach. It is important that the leader is greased in nymph fishing, so that it will give an indication of what is happening to the fly beneath the surface. The other basic difference is that drag does not matter quite so much when nymph fishing, in fact it may be a distinct advantage on a few occasions. However, it should never be ignored and should be avoided if possible.

A trout feeding beneath the surface, if visible, will be apparent not so much by movement but by the white of its mouth which shows as it opens and closes on food. Another indication of a fish feeding on nymphs is a swirl at the surface as it turns on some form of food. The trout should be stalked, as with dry fly, and casting should be just as careful, with the depth at which the fish is feeding taken into consideration before the cast is made. The fly should be cast sufficiently upstream to allow it to have reached the correct depth by the time it reaches the fish. Many fish will only take food as it reaches a particular point, sometimes rising in the water to do so but often requiring it at exactly the depth at which they lie. This is when the weighted nymph becomes useful in faster water. By using a nymph that is visible to the eye of the angler as well as to the fish simplifies matters greatly, because the progress of the fly can be watched, and if a fish takes hold, it will be seen. However, if this is not possible, the greased leader takes over as the next best way of telling what is happening to the fly. By casting over the fish, or likely lie, the fly hopefully sinks to the required depth and is propelled downstream simultaneously by the current. The leader, being greased, lies on the surface, and should be visible to the angler. The leader should be tight to the fly, so that if the fly is taken it shows immediately. A line which is clearly visible will not be detrimental to fishing, and if the leader does sink, then straightening the fly-line as it comes downstream will provide indication of takes in the same way that a greased leader would. The fly-line should be gathered in at least at the same speed as the current, as the fly travels downstream. Takes are indicated usually by the leader or fly-line shooting briefly forward and the strike should be instant and firm in those cases when the the fish has confidently taken the fly. Often the take comes simply as the halting of the downstream progress of the line and in this case also the line should be lifted firmly.

The best and most likely places to fish 'blind' for trout in running water are between streamer weeds, in eddies and in deep pools, particularly those formed by hatches (boards across the stream to regulate flow) in chalk streams.

When fish are known to be lying hard on the bottom of the stream or river and in deep water in particular, I find a shrimp pattern to be very successful. The pattern is attributed to the late Richard Walker, and I have used it to devastating effect in autumn on rivers. It is weighted by tying strips of lead along the back of the hook (about size 12), and a hump can be made; the body is of amber seal fur, with a palmered ginger cock hackle along its full length, ribbed with gold tinsel, the hackles are trimmed off along the back. The fly fishes upside down, due to the lead on the back of the hook, and it looks like a shrimp being carried downstream on its back, as they do. The other advantage is that the upside-down stance of the fly means that it actually rides over weeds. The lead can be as much as is required to make the fly sink to the necessary depth, or hug the bottom, and it is preferable to have flies of different weights in the box. Cast upstream, and fished just with the current, this fly can be deadly, but when it is moved it seems to lose its appeal. If it is fished in a deep pool where the current is slack, it should be retrieved in very short jerks until it is out of the pool. To pull a shrimp through a pool which contains fish will alarm them, and they can be seen to scatter around the pool. If this happens, the pool should be rested.

Although a shrimp pulled through the water does not seem to be successful, nymph fishing can produce an induced take. The induced take is very important in waters where the fish feeding on nymphs is under constant observation, and fishing for these can be enthralling and exciting.

Sometimes a nymph can be presented correctly to a fish as it feeds in midwater or lower, almost touching its nose as it passes. It may be ignored, but the fish continues to feed and can be seen to be doing so by movements to and fro across the river for short distances. If the fish refuses the nymph offered at what is judged to be the correct presentation, and refuses subsequent patterns (it should not be necessary to try many patterns) or sizes, then it may be that the induced take will produce the required results. If the fish cannot be seen, but it is known to be in a particular position, it can still be induced, but it is most exciting when the fish can actually be seen to be fooled into taking the fly.

The nymph is cast upstream of the fish and is allowed to sink to the depth at which the fish is feeding, as the nymph approaches the fish, the rod tip is raised, smoothly, so that the fly commences an upward journey to the surface, past the nose of the fish. The fish senses that it is about to lose a possible meal and makes a grab at the fly, becoming hooked in the process.

Those, then are the basics of the induced take and any feeding fish is likely to be duped into taking a nymph rising past it through the water. In practice it may not be so simple. The fish may ignore the fly, in which case the nymph should be pulled up from a number of positions, not just in front of the fish but from one side or another. The upward journey of the fly should never start too far upstream or the fish is likely to be alarmed.

It may be that the fish indicates an interest in the fly by moving momentarily in the right direction and returning to station again. If this is the case, the induced take should be repeated again and again until the fish is certainly not going to take. Often it will show increasing interest until it will eventually take. If it does not take immediately but shows interest, a change in patterns or size may produce results, but the next pattern tried should be something like the previous one, in either shape or colouring. It is always helpful if the nymph is visible to the angler when practising the induced take, but it is not essential as the leader always gives quite a clear indication of where the fly is. Pheasant Tail Nymphs with a coloured thorax can be particularly helpful in this respect—and effective.

As the winter draws closer, the weed will start to diminish with the cooling of the water, and the trout tend to withdraw into the deeper water. It is in this deeper water that leaded nymphs will prove to be more useful than unweighted patterns, and the induced take will become very effective. The fact that a fish does not show immediate interest in the fly does not mean that it will never do so. I once fished for a large rainbow trout in a deep pool in a chalk stream for more than twenty minutes before it eventually took the fly, downstream from where it had been lying, having turned and chased the fly. If the fish does turn onto the fly as it is being induced, the fly should continue the upward journey. To stop the lift of the rod tip will mean that the fish will in many cases instantly lose interest and may not look at that pattern again, or worse still may not look at anything again.

Throughout the autumn period the fish will occasionally rise to the dry fly, and may be taken readily on wet fly, but overall the nymph, when fished correctly, will usually take the most fish.

At the back end of the trout season, rainbows in particular can be seen agitating the bed of the stream and collecting together. These fish are going through the motions of breeding and should be left strictly alone. If caught, they will not provide good eating due to lack of condition. They are best left to recover their condition and in the following season they will provide excellent sport and be worth catching.

WINTER: GRAYLING

During the winter months, trout fishing is closed and rightly so, due to the lack of condition of the fish. They become dark in colour and lean, and are not worthy of capture because they make poor eating and because they do not provide real sport. However, in some parts of the country the flyfisherman can still find sport, if he feels the need in the bitter weather, in the form of the grayling. Grayling are graceful fish and are regarded as vermin on many trout streams. Because of their tendency to breed alongside coarse fish in terms of season, they are still available to be caught on the fly in winter. They possess the adipose fin that distinguishes game fish from coarse fish, and also provide excellent eating, and they can be exceptionally difficult to tempt on a fly although they will continue to rise. They are not as widespread as trout, but will rise to a fly throughout the year, although the larger specimens tend to stay deep.

Once hooked, the grayling needs careful playing to bring it to the net.

Three fine grayling that are above average size.

Grayling may be fished for during summer and autumn as well as winter, but many flyfishermen disregard them in favour of the trout. Grayling are very wary fish, and where they are present in a river which holds trout, they become alarmed earlier than trout and so must be treated with the utmost caution.

There is really nothing to add about grayling fishing methods to what has already been said for trout. They respond very well to the induced take, but great care must be taken because a shoal is being covered, and not just an individual fish as is often the case with trout. A hefty grayling is certainly a fish to be proud of and on fly tackle will fight every bit as hard as most trout, using its sail-type dorsal fin in the current.

PART III
SEA FISHING

Shore fishing

Boat fishing

Shore fishing

SPRING: DABS, FLOUNDERS AND PLAICE

Flounders have a somewhat tough time: they do not grow big, they are not fighters, and they follow the run of winter cod. Along the south coast, the cod season peaks around Christmas when the big fish feed hard, close to land, before being driven off by bitter weather and the urge to spawn. These shoals can sometimes be very large, with anglers scoring large bags trip after trip when they are present. Flounders fill the vacuum. Dab fishing is good around Christmas time, too. These tasty little flatfish do a public relations exercise in reminding shore fishermen that big may be beautiful, but small is succulent. While the titled—and monied—gentry goes fox-hunting on Boxing day, shore anglers go in search of dabs.

As well as being worthwhile fish to catch in their own right, small plaice, flounders and dabs make excellent baits for large bass in some parts of southern England, and can be float-fished over rocks for pollack, so it can prove to be worth the angler's while getting to know areas where these tiddlers are to be caught. This was vividly demonstrated one afternoon at a local jetty. A turbot suddenly appeared close to the structure and swam along it, near the surface and only a few feet out. Anglers tried jigging feathers in front of its nose, but it was not interested (curiously, nobody tried to foul-hook it). However, a tiny postage-stamp size plaice was trapped in the water's surface film. The turbot cruised up to it, opened its mouth and sipped in the tiny morsel.

Dabs

Few fish are as obliging as dabs. Their tastes range over a wide spectrum of baits—fish strips, soft crab and worms. Recently I was trying to catch them on peeled crab legs. Another hook on my trace was baited with mackerel strip. The dabs ignored the crab every cast. However, the very best bait of all for these obliging fish is stale black lugworm. If you have a few gutted worms left over after a cod trip, wrap them well in dry newspaper (and, if the paper becomes damp, rewrap them) and store them in a cool place. Within a week the worms will become tough strips of liquorice to look at and, to dabs, to eat.

You'll find them on fairly shallow beaches at this time of year, and not too far out. Most times they are to be caught where the shingle joins the sand of a moderately-deep beach. Long traces aren't needed—a two or three hook paternoster is ample to catch them two or three at a time.

Flounders

After the dabs, flounders come into their own. Although plenty of flounders are to be found in the sea during the cod season, the major run begins early in the New Year when the fish migrate down rivers prior to spawning in the sea. They fan out along the coast, the heaviest populations being found on sandy beaches close to their home estuaries. In some areas the fish move along the coast a short way before turning out to sea. Sometimes it pays to keep an ear open for the catches of other anglers so that you know the spot the groups have reached on their journey.

Ideal conditions at this time of the year arise in the aftermath of a storm. Flounders are suckers for shellfish. When a big wind has set up a heavy sea that ploughs up the bottom, digging out razorfish, butterfish and similar delicacies, the flounders move in en masse to feed on the abundance of smashed molluscs. They will then only rarely look at a lugworm, even though these will be washed in along with the shellfish.

Not every stretch of coastline offers these opportunities. It pays to find out where such a situation frequently arises. It also pays to explore the beach thoroughly in advance. Even fairly flat, sandy beaches have features that attract flounders. They love channels and depressions, especially those that run along the beach, parallel to the tide-line. The ones which will hold fish are also those that attract flotsam and jetsam. Bits of weed, old shells, waterlogged sticks and so on, do not settle in one place for no reason. And such places are also where the tides and eddying inshore currents deposit food. There is one such shallow depression on a beach near my home, which is a sure bet for gathering disorientated razorfish after a big storm. Anglers make sure that they cast into it when the tide has covered it, and make good hauls of whiting, flounders and codling. If the cast misses this depression—and it is only a couple of feet lower than the surrounding sand banks—catches will not be so great. Obviously the sea has positioned natural groundbait out there, so the wise angler exploits this situation. He can also groundbait such areas himself by hurling in well-punctured cans of fish-based catfood.

Fishing a sheltered estuary for flounders at dusk.

In order to ensure that casting is accurate, many anglers cast out to such areas at low tide. With the tackle correctly placed, they make any allowance that is necessary for the line-bowing effects of wind and current, then mark the line. The most effective way of doing this is to cut the line and knot it at that point. If you prefer, make a whipping of elastic thread at that point. With practice it becomes easy to judge how much power to put into each cast so that the hot-spot is located without having to reel in to the marker. Needless to say, match anglers make full use of these tactics.

In the absence of a handy storm, the angler has to make his own luck. Flounder fishing has become a precision art over the past few years because the species is a staple of the match angler. In the calm, settled seas that characterize much early-season sea fishing, the flounders will not be actively hunting out

food items. They will have reverted to their standard method of feeding, which becomes obvious when you examine the physical appearance of the flat-fish tribe. They hide in the sand, fluffing it around them to camouflage themselves against the attentions of predators and against the wariness of their prey. With their eyes set high up on their heads, they are able to view the world through virtually 360°, and take note of everything that happens around them.

Two tactics which work well are variations on a theme. The angler's task is to arouse the fish's interest by attracting its attention to his bait. One trick is to tie a peeler crab to one hook of a long trace and bait the other hook with red or white ragworm. Not big worms, but little ones that can be mounted on the hook in bunches and which will wriggle strongly. The flounders are attracted by the scent of the crab—a food that has strong appeal to them. When investigating the source of the delicious aroma, they come across a writhing bunch of ragworm—which also appeals strongly. One reason why white ragworm is so effective must be that it stands out well against the sea-bed. Red ragworm are slightly brownish in colour and do not contrast so well with the sand. When match fishing, the winner is very often the person who has spent much time digging for good white wrigglers.

Another tactic, which is effective in clear water, is to fix a button, a plastic teaspoon or coloured beads a few inches ahead of the bait. These are slowly retrieved across the bottom, 1 yd (1 m) at a time with a moderate pause in between. The fish grows curious and swims over to investigate. It finds the bait, and next time the angler starts to wind in, he will feel either a weight there, or maybe the bump of a fish trying to make off with the bait.

In some estuaries it is possible to float-fish for the flounders. On my local river the best time for this occurs when the tide is ebbing, but it varies from venue to venue. For maximum sport, try using roach-fishing tackle. Fine lines, small floats and split shot may not be standard items in the sea angler's armoury, but they are nonetheless effective when used in the right place at the right time. A bunch of harbour ragworm can be used in moving water, especially if the bottom is very dark and shows them up well. Set the float so that it fishes over-depth, with the lead shot a few inches up off the bottom. The current will then trundle the bait over the bottom and curious flounders will be moved to investigate.

This tactic works very well in late spring when the fish are moving back from spawning and are migrating up-river. The warm water makes the fish more active and they can even put up what I shall kindly describe as a fight.

Just to give you some idea of how rewarding it can be to base your tactics on the curiosity of flounders, a recent local match was won with twenty-two fish by an angler who float-fished with delicate tackle. Other anglers who used standard beach tackle and leger weights either caught nothing or just the odd fish.

Similar tactics can be very rewarding from a drifting boat. The best place to try this is in a very big estuary, especially one that dries out over much of its width at low tide. The flounders will then be concentrated in the deep channels. As the tide rises, the fish move out to explore the rapidly-submerging sandbanks. Flounders are not bothered by shallow water. Kids fish for them in silted-up drains alongside tidal rivers where the depth is rarely more than a couple of feet. Even here the fish will be lying close in at the sides of these drains, often with the water just covering their backs. Many anglers have trodden on flounders while wading out in surf in pursuit of bass.

When drifting estuary channels, try to get going before low tide so that the flooding tide carries you back to where you started. However, even in these apparently featureless channels there are places where the fish group up. These waters are the home of baited-spoon fishing. A plastic or metal spoon is fished ahead of a bunch or ragworms or a peeler crab. Flounders lie facing into the current, so it pays to drift with the tide, hoping that there is no wind to foul things up by pushing you off-course. They will see the spoon coming for some way and will move to intercept it. Larger-than-average fish are taken by such tactics.

This species is likely to turn up in a great variety of locations other than those listed above. I have caught them while plaice fishing several miles from land. And coarse fishermen regularly catch them on worms many miles up from the sea.

Although they bite best during the hours of daylight, a few are taken at night on strongly-scented baits like lugworms and razorfish. I recall once reeling in a flounder and a codling on the same hook. The flounder had taken the bait first and had managed to eject the hook through its gill-cover. A codling which attacked the worm hanging from the flounder's mouth—and I was using big cod baits and 4/0 hooks—somehow managed to become hooked in the back.

Flounders are not the tastiest of fish. Those that inhabit muddy locations tend to taste terrible. Open-sea flounders taste better, but not as good as plaice or dabs. And when they have finished spawning around early April, the spent fish have all the appeal of cotton-wool soaked in muddy water.

Right *A good catch of dabs and codling.*

7 lb (3 kg) of plaice caught on a whole fillet of mackerel from the Skerries bank, off Dartmouth.

Plaice

A large plaice is a handsome beast: large specks of orange, a broad back and thick across the middle. Such a fish is guaranteed to sparkle in the pan. And, when hooked on appropriate tackle, these fish give a good account of themselves.

They move inshore around March and can be caught in fair numbers from some beaches. The precise location of such places tends to be a well-kept secret because this species is a valuable commercial fish and anglers do not want to arrive at a favourite mark only to find that a cowboy netsman has festooned the area with trammels.

Lugworms and shellfish make the best baits, cast out on moderately light tackle. In some areas the fish move close to shore only after spawning, when they are spent and in poor condition. By the time they have recovered, they are usually feeding over mussel beds and off-shore sand-banks.

Mussel beds are a favourite home for plaice, even those that lie close in to the beach. However, many large specimens spend their lives quite unmolested by anglers or netsmen. They live in patches of mixed reef and sand where anglers rarely fish with the right baits and where netsmen are nervous about setting their gear. Often the only indication of their presence is when one is hooked unexpectedly.

For some reason anglers in all parts of the UK tend to ignore what is going on in other parts of the country. Plaice fishing is very popular in some areas with anglers who fish among rocky ground. Yet in other locations there are just as many plaice, but no anglers bother with them. This was brought home to me recently while chatting with an elderly angler in a pub. He had retired from the sport—his arthritis denied him youth's agility—and nobody else now fished the marks that he had discovered in his youth. He described them to me as large pockets of sand among the rocks. If you did not know they were there, you would think that only rock and rubble extended out to sea from the shoreline. These places are well off the main trawling grounds, being so close to shore, and he used to catch good fish from them.

Unfortunately he has since died, taking to the grave a vast store of shore-fishing lore. Regrettably I didn't take as much notice as I should have done to the precise marks he used to fish. But I found one the other day while trolling close into the shore over a bass reef. The water was as clear as tap-water and even without polarised glasses I could make out the sand. It was a broad, oval patch—about the size of a football field, hedged in by low rocks. There just had to be plaice down there. Such places are worth knowing because

the fish are allowed time to grow big. That is how I took a 4¾ lb (2.1 kg) fish one evening from a rocky mark.

To my mind the very best locations for sporting plaice fishing have to be piers. These fish dive if allowed to, and put up a fair scrap. Ideal tackle is a light spinning rod, fine line and a freshwater fixed-spool reel. Besides catching plaice, you will discover the delights of hooking gurnards, soles, whiting and other tiddlers on light tackle. They, too, will pull a bit. Even pouting have been known to struggle.

Some of the very best plaice fishing is to be found off shore. Sandbanks off Ramsgate give good sport in July while those off Dartmouth—the Skerries—fish best from March to May. Tactics for each bank are completely different. Ramsgate fish will take worms and shellfish on flowing traces, while the Dartmouth fish take a curious cocktail that looks like a stylized tadpole. First a peeler crab is tied to the hook with elastic thread, then a very thin and long strip of squid is tied alongside. This is trotted back behind the boat on a 6 lb or 12 lb (2.7 kg or 5.4 kg) class outfit. The bait is left lying for five minutes at a time, before being trotted back even further.

Sandbank plaice live on the slopes of the banks facing away from the tide. This is where food drops out of the current towards them, and where sand-eels take shelter. Plaice catch sand-eels quite efficiently and it seems as though the bait appeals to this aspect of their feeding characteristics.

Another tactic that works for off-shore plaice is the baited-spoon rig, although slow tides are required for it to be effective. Sheltered harbours, Scottish sea lochs and large estuaries are favoured plaice grounds. In these are to be found the gentle currents that help fish a baited spoon at the right speed. Plaice are not, after all, built for tearing around the ocean like mackerel. However all is not lost if the current is strong.

The trick here is to drift the bait a short while, then slip the reel out of gear and leave the bait lying on the sea bed for five minutes, letting out line rather than towing the tackle over the bottom. Put the reel into gear and if there is no resistance, either reel in and start again or drag the bait for a short while before leaving it be once more. Very often a plain sinker is as effective as a baited spoon for attracting the fish's attention.

One of the tragedies of the severe over-fishing that is taking place around our islands is the depletion of plaice stocks. Years ago this species used to feature strongly in shore catches everywhere. But the fish is neither a fast grower nor a fecund breeder: two qualities that are essential to survive prolonged depredation. So plaice are now a rare bonus for many shore anglers.

SUMMER: BASS

The regular bass areas are around the lower halves of England and Ireland. Stragglers are caught elsewhere, but consistent results are confined to the southern coasts. They move inshore when the water warms up in May and leave again in November. Where they overwinter, nobody is sure. Neither are we sure where they spawn, though tide races in April to July hold shoals of ripe fish. Much depends on the locality.

No fish so handsomely repays skill and dedication. The ham-fisted and non-specialist anglers catch a fair few each year, but specialization is the key to satisfaction. In this chapter, I am going to be whole-heartedly parochial and describe tricks and techniques that have paid off for me. It is then up to you to survey your local patch to see if there are any corresponding locations where you would estimate your chances of success to be high.

Some areas are famous for their big bass—others are populated mainly by small fish. However, that is outside the scope of this section. I will take you through my bassing season.

It starts on the surf beaches—and can end there. In March, April and autumn, bass congregate on Irish and south-western storm beaches where huge Atlantic breakers spend themselves on clean sand. The water is rarely coloured. If it is dirty, the bass stay outside in the cleaner water. If there is a moderate surf—not one that howls ashore with a deafening roar—the bass will be inside the breakers, feeding on shrimps, sand-eels, swimming crabs and suchlike along a narrow band that is brought about by two factors. First, the spent waves rush shorewards, pushing food ahead. Then the water runs back down the beach towards the breakers. You should place your baits, where the two forces meet. Lugworm, sand-eel and crab score best. Really fresh squid and mackerel are excellent baits for outsize specimens. Chest-high waders are advisable because when a wall of water bangs into your knees, it has enough energy to slop up over the tops of ordinary waders. Otherwise, good overtrousers should be worn. If you do ship water down inside your waders, they can be dried very swiftly with a hair-drier fitted with a wide flexible plastic pipe that, when slipped over the drier, directs the warm air down to the toes. Thoroughly soaked waders can be dried within half an hour with this technique.

Bass everywhere have their times, tides and weather. Local intelligence is vital unless you have inexhaustible patience. Even old hands dislike spending hours fishing empty water. Your best bet is to find out when the fish are feeding, and at what stage of the tide the shoals are likely to come through. With so much commercial pressure on bass at the moment, it is unlikely that you will be able to glean much information from local anglers just by walking up and asking them. You will get plenty of funny, and sometimes threatening looks and quite possibly will be sent hunting in the wrong direction.

My technique is to find which pub the locals gather in and buy a few rounds before broaching the question. This trick works no matter what species you are after. The secret is to use your brain to work out some obvious points, and then ask questions in such a way as to suggest that you know pretty well all there is to know, lulling the local expert into believing that he will not be giving too much away when he supplies a vital tit-bit of information. Do not ask 'What state of tide do the bass come through at Fermoyle?', but 'I have always had best results around low water up to half flood at Fermoyle—just the odd schoolie after that. Is that how you find it?' Anglers, even the secretive ones, seem unable to resist swapping experiences. Once he starts talking, do not interrupt him. Try to make sure he is not distracted by having an empty glass when 'last orders' is called.

One common mistake made in surf fishing is casting too far. The feeding zone is not so clearly fixed when there is very little wave action, so bass may be as far out as you can cast, but only under those conditions. Another mistake is to stand ground after casting when the line enters the sea at an angle. For sensitive bite indication, it is essential that the walls of water run up the line, and do not try to push a bow of line ahead of them. If this does happen, line will be forever pinging off the waves as they pass. Walk along the beach after casting so that the line enters the sea at right angles to it, offering least resistance.

Another mistake is to horse fish through the shallows when a wave is sluicing back down the sand. The pressure on the hook-hold is then at its greatest. Lightly-hooked fish will be torn free by the pressure of water. So slacken off the reel drag and, if the pressure becomes too great, let the fish take a controlled amount of line. Reel in fast and run backwards to regain line when the next water table comes rushing towards you, so that it carries the bass in to your feet. Careful play allows you to beach the fish with the least trouble. This trick is vital to all beach fishing. I have not carried a net or gaff for years, not even for cod or rays. Tackle should be light: an 11½ ft (3.50 m) rod casting 2–3 oz (60–90 g); a small reel with 10–12 lb (4.50–5.50 kg) line; a casting leader and fine wire hooks.

Storm-beach bassing often takes place under magnificent scenic conditions. By wading out in the water, less line is out, so bites are felt more easily. And, most

When rock fishing for bass, watch out for the tide.

The moment of release. Note that the reel spool is revolving fast enough to throw out spray – yet the rod is barely straight.

important of all, the angler becomes part of the scenery. Sport can be magical when fish are running well.

However, rock fishing is best of all. Each patch of southern reef is well-known to bass anglers. They spend hours over the years charting the progress of bass shoals along certain parts of the coast. At low tide, they may be milling in an eddy, say, off a small nose of rock. Then, as the tide starts pushing, they will make their way along the coast. The angler comes to understand that he will have time for maybe two casts into a certain gully, then a quarter-mile walk to a jumble of fallen boulders, where he stands another chance of intercepting the feeding fish. Sadly, trammel netters today can place a murderous, invisible web across these feeding routes and wipe out the inshore stock of fish within a couple of days. Little wonder that bass anglers habitually wreck any trammel nets they find.

Rock fishing is essentially crab fishing. Nothing can beat a velvet swimming crab that is just minutes away from shucking its shell when you turn over the rock under which it is hiding. If none of these magnificent

and pugnacious critters are to be found along your shoreline, then edible crabs are the ones to use. Failing them, use green-backed shore crabs. Edibles and velvets exude sticky juice when peeled that clogs up the soft skin between your fingers. It is this juiciness that wafts through the weeds and rock gullies to advertize the presence of your bait. That is why bass anglers lash on their baits with any colour of elastic thread they have to hand, and why they are not in the least bit bothered by the final appearance of the bait. Provided it is match-box size and oozing juice, it fits the bill.

When crabs are scarce, try peeling legs and claws and lashing them together in bundles with thread. It is the scent that matters. If the crab is still fairly meaty-looking when you reel it in, squeeze it between forefinger and thumb to release more attractive juices. If crabs are small, tie them on in bundles of three or four. All angles have to be explored if you are to place an attractive bait out there.

An essential trick when casting into heavy graunch is to not tighten the line unless it is very slack. Wind and tide should do that for you. The sinker and bait should not be budged from where they settle for fear of dragging them into a crevice, or of the hook catching round a weed stem. After years of practice, you will learn to detect whether or not you are snagged from the way waves move the rod-top. The line feels harder than it should do. Under very snaggy conditions, tackle up with 22 lb (10 kg) main line with 16 lb (7 kg) to the hook and just 5 lb (2.25 kg) to the tiny leads, which are quite adequate. If there is no tide, a ¾ oz (22 g) bomb will suffice. If there is a fair current, go up to 2 oz (60 g), but never any more. The same rod and reel can be used as is suitable for the surf—fast-taper, fine-tipped and it should be both lightweight and well balanced for long periods of use.

Long traces are anathema in both surf and graunch. In surf they tangle round the main line. Among rocks they entwine the weeds and boulders. Also, any crabs that are picking at the bait will retreat with the baited hook under cover and thus snag you. That is why lighter line is preferable, so that the main line does not break when you have to snap out of a snag. The 22 lb (10 kg) line is better at coping with flints and barnacles. Very often the bait will be lying the other side of a ledge and when the fish takes, it will chafe the line. Strong line will not break, but even so, it should be wound back through fingers to check for damage after each cast. Suspect areas must be cut out or you risk losing a large fish. It is bound to happen. The way to guarantee hooking into a very big fish is to use weakened tackle. It is as sure a system as the bassman's method of inducing takes when very little seems to be happening out there. Put the rod down to fumble for a cigarette or to pour a coffee, and the tip will go whanging over as a good bass hits and runs.

Concentration is vital because when a bass takes the bait you must react correctly to it. Most takes consist of a knock or two followed by a good pull. Sometimes the fish just knock and then you get a nibbling sensation: strike. Or it may be a slack-liner which requires you to reel like a lunatic so as to tighten the line and effect a hook-setting strike.

Weather for rock bassing is as variable as prime locations. Rough water on the rocks will give you fish in some areas, while in other places the bass hate such conditions and will bite only when the sea is flat. About the only consistent factor that I have found is that bass rarely feed in mud holes among rocks where sea-borne rubbish accumulates. They prefer to feel the tide in their faces and will only enter gullies when water is flowing through them.

Bass can be found among rocks in May through to July. If the weather warms up to the extent that sprats, mackerel, smelt and similar forage fish become abundant, the bass move off-shore or to deeper-water beaches. If you have a boat and live in the right area, large hauls of bass can be made in July when they gang up on forage fish. Flocks of frenzied gulls give away their presence. Catches under such conditions can be measured in hundredweights. Sadly many anglers have been beguiled by the price bass fetch in the market-place and kill all they catch. This is folly. A 7 lb (3 kg) female is about twenty years old. Severely-hammered stocks take decades to recover. Sportsmen should bear this in mind before clouting everything on the head and reckoning up their day's takings on their pocket calculators.

While pirks and large cod feathers slaughter the fish under these circumstances, more fun can be had from fish-feeding bass by trolling slowly over the reefs where they lie in ambush, waiting to pounce on unsuspecting tiddlers. Very large fish are caught at these times by people with small boats working over the rocks, losing the occasional redgill sand-eel in the process, because fry-feeding bass prefer to work very close to the sea-bed. Quiet engines are vital to success.

Another trick that works at night from steep-to shingle beaches that characterize many resort seafronts is this. Catch some baby pouting and drop them 5–10 yd (5–10 m) out at high tide. Bass come in to feed on the old sandwich crusts left behind by tourists and missed by the gulls. They also take baby pouting that have not survived being torn off the hooks by holiday anglers. They work in very close, provided the sea is calm and clear. This trick is carried to sophisticated lengths in some parts of the world. Small fish like mackerel, herrings, sprats, launce, whiting and pouting are 'junkied' by injecting the swim-bladder with a hypodermic syringe full of air to make them float. This works from piers, breakwaters and other quiet corners. However, the fish must be expecting to find such fodder in those places. A surf beach is not the right place to try this, although it might work. In fishing, you never know until you have tried it.

Dead and live pouting can be float-fished from piers, trotted down estuaries on the tide or legered on the bottom. Very big bass are most partial to pouting. This writer should know. The second bass he ever caught weighed 8¾ lb (4 kg) and fell to a badly-hacked fillet of pouting. Very big fish are taken on such baits from rock marks, too, especially late in the year, around September.

Live fish are best in clear water. They do not like being fixed to hooks and will flicker in panic when a predator is detected. It senses the vibrations and distress of the bait fish and launches an attack.

In some estuaries and marinas, July is the time when smelt take over. When boats enter or leave harbour, they churn up the little baitfish in their screws and flocks of gulls and terns dine well on easy pickings. Bass will be about when the daylight activity quietens down or before it begins. It pays to obtain a large bucket—a 10 gal wine-makers' vat—and fit it with a portable aerator. Remember, though, that 10 gal weighs 100 lb (45 kg). This size prevents fish flipping

Above *A good bass, but many anglers are worried for the chances of others surviving the eighteen years required to reach this size.*

Right *Fly-fishing for estuary bass is hectic when schoolies shoal up at dusk during high summer.*

out onto the road, as you carry it to the bass-fishing location only partially full.

Very light tackle can be used in many estuaries. Gear that is suitable for chub will be effective against the school bass that are normally expected. And a big fish will provide vivid flash-backs for years ahead. If the bottom is not too snaggy, a killing method is as follows. Make up a leger tackle with about 4 ft (1.2 m) to the hook and 2 ft (60 cm) to the sinker. A light-weight lead allows you to trot the baitfish back with the tide, keeping it close to the sea-bed, where it will most readily be detected by feeding bass and where it is less likely to drown in the full force of the current. As much of this activity takes place at night, a float will prove hard to see even in well-lit harbours, and the angler constantly needs to retrieve his bait out of the tide-run, which will not do it any good. Livebaits should always be lively.

Perfection for this writer at this time of the year is fly-fishing. Bass often gang up where a tidal current boils over a reef, where an estuary outflow hits the sea, and in many other places where fast water is suddenly halted by either still water or a more solid feature. At estuary mouths, small fish carried down in the current will be jostled head-over-tail-fin in the confused over-falls and are easy prey to the bass, mackerel and other predators that hang about waiting for the feed to come down to them on the ebb. There is an excellent reason why this should be so. Tides flowing up estuaries take with them billions of gallons of sea-water. This water is full of fry when they are close to shore in summer. When the estuary debouches its water into the sea, these fry come with it. This is why beaches inside estuaries are so often smothered with drift-wood.

All you need do is to arm yourself with a fly rod of reservoir lure-casting proportions, a suitable reel that will not rot to pieces after a season's use in saltwater (being alloy, regular washing and cleaning is essential), and AFTM 9 shooting-heads. Much depends on the depth of the water when estimating what line to use. In skinny water, use a floating or slow-sinking line. In deep water, a fast-sinker or even a lead-core. The sole criterion is the depth at which the fish are hunting. Often schoolies can be seen splashing at the surface. Many anglers go for those, unaware that larger specimens may be feeding underneath. Lures should be tied on size 2 and 4 hooks, with combinations of silver, white and blue in the feather or hair-wing dressings. A slash of red hackle at the throat can provoke an attack. After dark, black lures stand out well. The fish are then likely to be deep with little surface splashing, silhouet-ting bait against the night sky.

You can also spin for bass in these and other locations. Lures cast out on fly tackle are more whimsical in their action than spinners, and while I have had countless bass follow metallic lures and red-gills in to my feet, I have always found that a following bass will suddenly accelerate and grab at a fly-type lure.

However, one vital piece of equipment should always be used by the flyfisher—a stripping basket. This is for the line to lie in as it is being retrieved. Without it, line dangles into the water and snags around stones and weed stems, making the next cast a total failure as a tangle of line loops and weed jams in the rod's butt ring.

Two points should be stressed here. The first is that ultra-clear water is essential to success. This is because the fish need to be able to see the lures if they are to strike at them. The second point is that small fish make up the bulk of catches. While there is nothing wrong with catching small bass, it is essential that a very high percentage be released if stocks are to survive. While the little fellows fight well on fly tackle, there is little chance of them falling off the hook if reasonable line-tension is maintained throughout the struggle, so barbless hooks are recommended. All you do is to take a file and carefully pare away the hook's barb. Thus small fish can easily be released without even removing them from the water. Just hold the fly and gently shake off the fish. It is a very satisfying sight to see a schoolie skidding through the shallows.

A small triangular file is an essential part of the sea-fisherman's tackle. It should be lightly smeared with grease—preferably a silicone compound as this is excellent at repelling water. Salt rots a file, blunting the cutting edge and a rusted file is useless for sharpening hooks. Few hooks are perfect as bought. A hook with a short, very sharp point is best for all fishing. Long points can bend and even snap if they strike into bone. A point that tapers rapidly is stronger. The barb should be small, for ease of penetration. Small barbs make unhooking easier, with less damage likely to the fish's mouth.

Bass can be hard to find during August. There is so much food out there in the form of small fish that predators do not have to work hard for their meals. A couple of small mackerel—ten minute's work in some places—fill the fish up for the day. But in September and towards winter, the fish fatten up for their winter fast, lining their body cavities with fat which will later be vital for the formation of roes. Very big fish are taken in autumn. Fish baits score well, though often there is a late flush of peelers in the rock-pools and bass will come looking for them. Autumn is also a good time on the storm beaches.

However, the bass is mainly a summer fish. It falls most readily to fishermen who are prepared resolutely to climb out of bed when the alarm clock goes off at four o'clock on a fine summer's morning. Moreover, much research is required to pin-point likely feeding areas, which vary from tiny patches of sea-bed no larger than the average back garden, up to vast sweeps of open beach.

Bass are somewhat unconventional in their habits. They will group together wherever the feeding is good. One such area is sewer outfalls and pipes that take food waste to sea. A friend catches good fish on large balls of cheese-paste cast out on light leger tackle close to a pier's restaurant. Swill is regularly tipped in here. This may be contrary to local bye-laws, but the fish are not concerned with such regulations. Like most fish, they are opportunists and their seasonal habits encompass a wide range of feeding sites.

Despite the high price that their flesh commands in restaurants throughout Europe, sea anglers regard bass as essentially a sport fish. Most dedicated bass men use tackle that is as light as possible for whatever environment the fish are feeding in. In heavy rock where lines may be snapped on barnacles and flints, 30 lb (14 kg) line may be used, but the rod will still be sensitive and supple. When bassing, there is rarely any need to take vast quantities of tackle. Often the man who travels with minimal gear and has maximum mobility will be the one who scores best during the season, and this in itself makes it appealing. However, the most important factor is that the best fishing takes place among some of the world's most spectacular oceanic scenery.

AUTUMN: RAYS

Of the fourteen species of skate and ray that are to be found around the British Isles, only a handful can be caught from the shore. The common skate—the true skate, not the fish and chip shop skate, which are rays—accounts for the vast majority of skate catches, with neither the long-nosed nor the white skates ever having been caught—to date—from the shore. Of the dozen or so ray species, the thornback makes up the bulk of catches, with the small-eyed ray the second most common. A few blonde and spotted rays are caught, mainly in localized areas. The same goes for that individualist, the sting ray. For practical purposes, this chapter is devoted to the common skate, the thornback (the most commonly-caught ray species) and the stinger. This categorization roughly separates the three different feeding habits of the tribe.

For those who are keen to see their name in the record books, it should be noted that a large number of record-sized rays have been incorrectly identified; often by boatmen who are not bothered because each species is as valuable as the next in the fish market.

Therefore plenty of would-be records have ended up gutted and cooked before the captor realized his error. Since the Record Fish Committee accepts only complete fish and not chunks cooked in batter, the would-be record seeker is advised to obtain one of the many books devoted to fish identification and study the differences. To do so here would be boring both for the reader and the author and, as is often the case, brief differentiation does not solve the problem. Only when different species are compared and contrasted against each other, with identification book in hand, do the dissimilarities become obvious and stick in the mind.

The ultimate shore-caught species have to be the porbeagle shark, common skate and tope in that order. Porbeagles can be caught from Ireland's wild Atlantic coastline, and several large skate have been caught there, too. In Ireland, large common skate have been caught from Fenit pier on Tralee Bay and Foynes pier on the Shannon Estuary. Other monsters have been caught from piers and deep-water rock marks off the west coast of Scotland. It is highly probable that others are there to be caught.

The problem facing the slayer of monsters is that these huge fish do nothing to give away their location. Deep water over a fairly smooth bottom of flat rock, sand, shingle and so on characterizes the likely swim in which they can be found. They are fairly territorial, as has been found out to their cost by the Irish Tourist Board. When skate fishing was fanfared some twenty years ago, many anglers went to places like Kinsale and caught huge bags, killing everything that came aboard the boats. But these slow-growing dinosaurs do not move around and repopulate fished-out areas, so catches dwindled. The ones that were out there had been caught, and fishing was destroyed in a very short space of time.

Because of this territorial nature—they tend to hunt round specific areas with the tide—it should be possible to locate likely shore fishing spots through research. Find out known skate grounds, especially ones that are close to land, and then sort out a likely shore station.

The success or failure of such a mission completes about one quarter of the research needed. After sorting through many miles of coastline for what strikes you as a likely spot, you must have immense patience, many blank days and disappointments, before a fish turns up—if one does. Groundbait can help here. Throw in quantities of fish offal, but be prepared to attract congers and dogfish as well.

With these tiddlers about you have to fish most attentively so that you know when a skate has taken the bait, and that the knocks and trembles on the rod-tip signify a skate and not a doggie pecking away

Idyllic conditions, but even so wrap up warmly as the weather can change very quickly.

down there. Skate are water-borne blankets and smother their prey. They then use the sensory organs in their skin to reposition themselves so that the prey can be engulfed by their mouths. All this takes time. So do you wait while a doggie messes about down there—and it can be hard to tell the difference—or do you reel in and replace the bait?

One way to get round the problem is to use large baits. A skate's mouth may look small when shut, but is of bucket-like proportions when fully open. A record-size mackerel would disappear inside that maw without touching the sides, so extra-large baits are likely to sort out skate from other fish. However, this is where single-minded determination comes in. By fishing one huge bait, inaction is likely to last for weeks. So, to while away the time and maintain some sort of interest in the proceedings, it may be wise to take along two rods and fish smaller baits for other fish on the second one, leaving 5 lb (2.2 kg) of squid to lie in one place all day.

When a big fish does materialize, many anglers are uncertain whether it is a skate or a boulder that has taken the bait. Anglers have broken out from skate, believing themselves to be snagged into the sea bed. However, careful searching of the sea bed with a lead weight (no hooks or bait) on your research expeditions should have shown you whether or not there is much likelihood of this happening.

One useful trick can be carried over from rock bass fishing. Here, with short distances being cast, the angler uses very light line to his sinker. So if he snags, he can lose the lead without having to heave on the rod. And sometimes such sinkers are lost on the strike. When skate fishing, a very large bait is used to interest the fish. So the attendant lead weight is no more than an anchor to prevent the bait drifting with the tide. With, say, a 30 lb (14 kg) main line and a running leger, 10 lb (4.50 kg) line can be used to fix on the sinker. If the hook is reasonably well buried into the bait—to prevent it snagging rather than to hinder its effectiveness on the strike—there should be little opportunity for the bait to snag. So, by following these thoughts and making suitable plans, the fish that gives you a trembling knock may be a skate. Do not break out of it. Keep heaving (a 10 ft [3.05 m] maximum rod is essential because a long one will work against you) until the skate moves or unsticks from the sea bed. How to proceed after this, I am not sure. Skate caught from piers have taken up to four hours to bring to gaff. You will be the pioneer, so it is something that will have to be sorted out according to the site where you will be fishing.

A gaff will, hopefully, prove to be essential when, after ten years of hunting, your barn-door-shaped Moby Dick hits the surface. A flying gaff would be ideal. This is a gaff with a barbed point, which has a head that can be removed from the pole. The head is held in place by a length of rope which is tied to it at one end, with the other fixed to a suitably firm anchorage. They are used extensively for tropical big-game fishing, with the rope tied to a part of the boat. The gaff head is wedged onto the pole and held there by gripping both pole and rope. Upon sinking the gaff, the pole is pulled clear and the fish is hauled up, thrashing and protesting, on the rope. This item of equipment can be used for a variety of tricky situations where large fish are encountered—congers, tope, cod—even rays.

Tackle for a giant shore skate would have to be very tough—line of at least 30 lb (14 kg) test—much heavier would be impossible to use because few anglers can impose more than about 25 lb (11 kg) of pressure—and that not as a sustained pull—onto a rod. The reel would be a low-geared multiplier, and it will have to be thumbed throughout the cast else the out-size bait will cause it to over-run. A fixed-spool reel could be used if one could be found that would stand up to the tremendous strains involved. It will have to be fitted with a roller rewind arm and not a standard bale arm, which would snap. Skate teeth are not too fierce, being crushing slabs rather than pointed, so heavy commercial nylon traces would be suitable, or, if they make you nervous, standard braided wire. Hooks would be 8/0–10/0, sharpened to a cutting edge on the barb and an ultra-sharp point for easy penetration.

Quite what you do after landing such a monster is hard to say. Skate deserve to be conserved and so ideally should be returned unharmed. However, the capture of one off the beach is so rare that it could be argued that slaughter is permissible under these circumstances.

Let us turn our attention now to more easily attained members of this group of selachians. While several species of ray can be caught from the shore, the majority are thornbacks. These are caught from a variety of grounds all round the British Isles. In some places they can be caught alongside different members of the group. Their feeding habits are similar (except for the sting ray, which will be dealt with separately).

The location of ray marks is largely a matter of paying attention to the angling press and keeping your ears waggling when you hear other anglers talk about them. They are less easily come by than of yore because trawling has proved to be so effective a means of keeping down their numbers. Recognized marks can be gathered from several where-to-go fishing books, though these are usually less helpful than they at first appear to be. Many ray marks require long walks, scrambles down cliffs, and precise location. As ever with this type of research, tackle dealers are your best bet once you have located a suitable area—or fishing clubs. But another, and generally more helpful, source of intelligence is crab and lobster potters. These men set their traps among heavy ground which rays do not particularly like, even though thornbacks can be found among reefs. They are likely to be able to tell you of marks where sand lies in deep water within casting range of rock ledges. These places are always likely ray marks, especially along the wilder parts of our coastline where the fish are less frequently disturbed.

Surf beaches like those on the Gower coast in Wales and Ireland's famous strands are also good bets for rays, especially during periods of calm weather when the fish will come in close. They dislike surf and stay out during rough water conditions.

Ideal weather conditions are hot, humid and flat calm. These fish respond best if the state of tide when they are most active coincides with dusk or dawn. They feed largely by scent, so night fishing with squid, frozen sand-eels, sprats, herring and, in some places, lugworm, is often the most productive.

Rays tend to move down the tide as they feed, travelling in small groups. If you get a series of runs, then nothing, it may pay you to move along the beach a short way to relocate the fish. Obviously such tactics work only in those areas that still experience a run of rays. Many areas offer patchy sport—two or three fish per week, and then only after long hours spent tending the rod. Rays, like most other sea fish, have fairly regular timetables, coming on to feed at one stage of tide, with another stage being no more than a waste of time.

Some of the best results come to anglers who fish over their spawning grounds. These appear to be inside large estuaries, where the baby fish can feed on the myriad life forms in sheltered water until large and bold enough to venture out to sea. Shrimpers who push nets close in on sandy beaches around such areas often catch immature rays. They make fascinating—and exquisitely graceful—additions to a saltwater aquarium.

Tactics for ray fishing are fairly basic. However, there is a trick which boat anglers use for thornbacks and which may be useful to the beach angler. In some parts of the country an attractor spoon is fixed close to the bait. Such terminal rigs often outfish standard legered baits. Rays do catch live fish, despite their somewhat ungainly appearance out of water, so perhaps the attractor appeals to this side of their character. However, few anglers have tried such rigs from the beach.

Most of the time, bottom-fishing techniques are used to catch rays. Long traces are a waste of time, especially since they muffle the initial bumps and trembles which signify that a ray is snuffling around the bait. Never be in too much of a hurry to strike a ray. It rarely lets go of a bait once it has tasted it. And it takes a long time to transfer the bait from the sea bed to its mouth. With its wings catching on the line, the angler is likely to see what looks like a pouting or billet pecking away at the bait. Experience at interpreting rod-tips' movements teaches the difference. Small fish give small tugs more frequently than investigative rays.

Eventually the bait will be taken fully into the fish's mouth and it will move off in search of somebody else's offering. Then is the time to strike. If you do so too soon you are likely to feel the fish there for a second, then nothing. Or you may foul-hook the fish in a wing—and such an uncertain hook-hold is likely to be insecure. Because of the hardness of the bed of bony pads that forms the ray's teeth, the hook has to be behind them before an effective strike is made. No standard beach-fishing rod can bang a hook through those crab-crushers. Your hook-point is likely to come back turned or snapped off.

Rays sometimes run when hooked, especially in clear shallow water. Most times the sensation is akin to heaving in a drowned polythene sack. Small-eyed rays are among the most active and can, at times, put up quite spirited resistance. Thornbacks often tail-tangle the trace and become so immobilized that they can offer no resistance at all, other than that of a dead weight.

Fishing for rays is very similar in many respects to fishing for cod. It is basically a matter of casting a big bait out a long way to where they feed, unless deep water comes close in to piers or rocks. Some of the best fishing is to be had from fairly flat, shallow beaches. It seems as though rays are aware that they are not built for speed and might be stranded if they were to come too close to the edge. So the shore fisherman needs the skill to cast out a long way. A standard ray fishing rod should be built with plenty of back-bone so that largish baits can be launched out to the feeding grounds. On several occasions I have noticed that long casters have scored while average performers have not had so much as one take.

So a meaty rod is required, not just to throw out baits but to haul the fish ashore. Sometimes it will try to bury itself in sand while being played. The angler can do no more than pile on maximum pressure and hope to persuade it to move. However, this is not easy because the angle between the angler and the fish is virtually nil, so he cannot lift it off the bottom. I have known anglers to break out after pressurizing a ray for ten to fifteen minutes with no result.

Thornback rays—one of several species available from British beaches.

The rod tip should be fine so that early warning is received of a fish's attention. The knocks—sometimes quite sharp—signify that a ray is out there. This advance notice is essential if the strike is to be timed correctly for sound hooking.

Long-casting reels, like the lightweight Ambassadeurs, are adequate for ray fishing. Rays are not runners so reserves of line are not essential. Besides, not even a tournament caster would be able to empty the spool of line when loaded up with a respectable bait.

For this reason it is wise to use a bait clip on the leader—and a streamlined paternoster tackle also—so that air resistance is reduced to a minimum. Bait clips also ensure that the bait is presented perfectly, looking as it did when it was lying in the palm of your hand.

Wire traces used to be popular with ray fishermen. They have now been discarded as unnecessary. Nylon of 30–40 lb (14–18 kg) is ample for the fish to chew on, and has been proved to be more effective than wire. Rays can be put off a bait by the hardness of metal.

Hooks should be tough, forged and of reliable temper. They take considerable strain. Good ones are O'Shaughnessy and Sundridge Specimen Longshank. Neither model can be crushed by ray teeth, nor will they spring open under pressure when a hooked fish goes to ground and the angler tries to shift it.

Years ago, when large numbers of rays were to be found inshore, anglers who fished beaches that dried out for a long way at low tide used to groundbait for their fish. They would anchor a sack full of rotting mussels and fish guts in the gullies and tide-ways along which feeding fish would be moving at high tide. Accurate casting was essential, and the old trick of marking the line at the right place, and fishing to that mark, was used extensively.

Although ray fishing can be very good in the autumn, especially for the larger specimens of small-eyed rays, this group of species is very fond of calm, warm water. So summer is also an excellent time for them, with the first fish appearing along the beaches when the crabs migrate inshore in the spring. However, some fair catches of rays are made in December from beaches in North Wales. As I said at the beginning—keep your ears and eyes open.

A point that is worth consideration here may not be to the liking of some sea anglers. Despite the undercurrent of enmity that exists between anglers and commercial fishermen, it has to be said that the commercial boys are out there virtually every day and know precisely what is moving, what is abundant, and what species are conspicuous through their absence. Fishmongers—and their slabs—often reveal a great deal about the current state of fish stocks. So if plenty of rays are offered for sale—or even if the local chippie is offering skate as 'today's special', the chances are that they are locally-caught. The best place for all angling intelligence is the local fish wholesaler or market. In some ports there exists a co-operative among the skippers, with one man or organization marketing the catch and charging them a small commission on sales, thus taking the burden off them so that they can spend more time doing what they are best at—catching fish. These are the people to contact because they receive reports from a wide range of fishermen, covering all types of grounds and virtually all methods of fishing.

One ray species stands out among all the other commonly-caught ones, and that is the sting ray. There are, in fact, two species in British waters, but the eagle ray is so rarely caught that it barely merits mention. Likewise that live wire, the electric ray, of which three species are to be found around the British Isles. Very few of these are caught each year, and then normally from boats.

The sting ray is a summer tourist, spending the warm months lazing in the sun on shallow-water coasts. Noted marks are Ireland's Tralee Bay, the Solent, Rustington, Worthing and the Thames Estuary. The species requires patient dedication and a certain amount of luck, so other areas undoubtedly exist, but have yet to be exploited by anglers with the right attitude. The fish grows very big in our waters—100 lb (45 kg) fish have been taken in trammel nets set over shallow grounds for mullet, flatfish and bass.

The sting ray is a powerful fighter, especially on light tackle.

It is a fairly conservative fish, preferring king ragworm and crabs to anything else, though it has been taken on lugworm and fish strips. As ever, different baits are preferred over different grounds, so the above list is far from exhaustive.

The trick in locating a stinger mark is to read the angling press and take note of the chance captures. These fish are caught by anglers who had other species in mind when they cast out their baits. Because the average shore stinger is about 40 lb (18 kg), such specimens are generally reported to the press. Besides, the fish makes an impression on its captor by being both an aggressive fighter, large, and a novel catch.

It also has an evil reputation. Its whip-like tail can inject venom into a wound, and should be avoided when a fish is landed, especially since the beast lashes it about. However, stingers are fairly easy to deal with. Flip the fish over onto its back with the butt of your rod. It will then be partially immobilized. Do not break off the sting—that is a barbaric practice. Indeed, stingers should be accorded a great deal of respect and careful attention when landed. The fish is comparatively rare, so should be returned to the water alive, to fight another day.

So little is known about the sting ray that the angler who goes out intent on catching them would be advised to obtain some Peterson tags from a marine fisheries laboratory—at Plymouth or Lowestoft, among others—and tag fish in the wing so that their migration patterns can be recorded. As the species is inedible, and therefore of no commercial value, no research has been undertaken into its life-cycle or migratory patterns. Marine scientists still have enough mysteries to solve with species like cod for them to waste time on sting rays.

The known facts have been supplied largely by anglers. The species likes shallow, sun-warmed water where it can be reached mainly through long-range casting with the baits mentioned above. Tackle and tactics are virtually the same as for other rays. Strong line is not necessary to haul the fish off the sea bed because it fights by running, often leaping and changing direction very rapidly. The sight of a big stinger breaking surface on a sun-drenched summer's day is likely to set the heart thumping and adrenalin coursing through one's cholesterol-choked veins.

Although stingers are inedible, other ray species can be eaten—if you have a taste for the boneless, slightly sweet fish. They should be bled for the table, skinned, and, some say, hung for a couple of days to improve the flavour. A degree of dexterity is required for converting a slimy, thorny ray into a succulent forkful of flavour. Novices are advised to contact their local fish-monger for a practical demonstration of this skill.

WINTER: COD

It is quite ridiculous, but in the heat of July many dedicated anglers become discontent with the surfeit of bass, tope, mullet and so on, and begin to dream of winter's whistling winds, grey, lumpy seas, and the arrival of cod. As with all branches of sea fishing, this has its own special flavour which, while it is happening, has anglers believing that there is nothing like it in the whole world; that is, until the first snows of the New Year set them dreaming about summer nights under the stars, soft crabs and broad-shouldered bass.

Winter cod fishing has an enormous following. Many coarse anglers swell the ranks of shore fishermen in pursuit of this prolific fish. The winter season can start as early as late August with the whiting shoals moving inshore. This gives everybody a chance to get sorted out, sharpen their casting skills, and mentally prepare themselves for long vigils in winter's damp and chilly darkness.

Shore fishing for cod is an art. Many anglers never quite manage to reach the high pitch that is vital for consistently good bags. Top performers often measure their catches in hundredweights at the end of a good season, with some tides producing huge bags of fish. This author's personal best in four hours fishing was seventeen cod weighing just over 1 cwt (50 kg); not bad sport from the shore. Of course, with such tremendous commercial pressure on this species, half of Europe being eager to eat it, bags have dwindled in the last twenty years. Although cod stocks have always been cyclic, the bags of 500–800 lb of fish that were recorded in the past between two or three anglers in one tide simply do not happen any more.

There are two types of winter cod beach—the steep-to shingle beach which gives on to a smooth, fairly clean sea-bed. And the heavy rock piles, ledges and scars of Yorkshire. Most British cod fishermen prefer to fish the open beaches. Yorkshire rock-hopping is limited to local interest since clean ground is lacking in those areas where the high Yorkshire Moors fall sheer into the sea.

Let us kick off with a look at open-beach cod fishing. This is popular around many parts of the south, west and east coasts. It is a somewhat basic form of fishing. The object is to cast a bait that cod like to eat out to where they are most likely to find it. This could be said for many other forms of shore fishing. However, in the case of cod, there is little to do other than that. Little subtlety is required because cod are voracious predators and fearlessly pounce on anything that takes their fancy. Bites consist of positive heaves on the rod-tip, quite unlike the delicate tugging of a bass feeding leisurely on soft crabs. Many rods are lost each year to cod which drag them into the sea while the owner is not paying attention.

So when is the best time to fish for cod? Much depends on the locality in which you will be operating. Around my home patch, the south-east coast, there is a fair run in October which peters out in November if there are not huge numbers of fish migrating around the coast. Peak season is the spring tides in December, with some of the best fishing being around Christmas. December fish are often very large. These are driven offshore when the sea temperature drops at the onset of severe weather in January. Only small fish remain. This is, of course, a generalization. Anglers will have a good session if a shoal of big fish comes by in January. However, here we are concerned with consistent patterns of behaviour.

Winter codding cannot compete, from the point of view of comfort, with balmy summer nights when the stars blaze down from a clear sky. The weather borders on the spiteful for much of the time. While modern clothing and tactics are effective at minimizing the effects of this weather, too much cold can jade your appetite for codding, and make you less keen to leave the fireside just when the big fish move in around December. There is no point in spending day after day and night after night scratching for the occasional fish. Use the grapevine, and concentrate on a few beaches to make sure that you hear about good catches as they happen. Tackle dealers are often very helpful. As their shops are central clearing houses for fishing intelligence, you can reach the stage where the dealer will telephone you when he thinks something good is about to happen. Of course, I am talking about a normal season in which the shoals gradually amass off the beaches, with catches becoming steadily more consistent as each day passes. If the fish are thin on the sea bed (cod stocks are erratic in this respect—two poor seasons can be followed by a bumper crop), the only effective tactic is to peg at it and trust that you are doing everything right when a few fish do come along the beach.

Certain skills and items of tackle are essential before you even put worm to water. Clothing requires priority attention. You need to be able to walk long distances, dig bait, and cast well in it. This rules out multi-layers of sweaters because wool is both heavy and inefficient when compared to modern thermally-efficient man-made fibres. The wise angler invests in a complete set of these, together with a set of well-made waterproofs and a pair of moon-boots. I have frequently fished in weather conditions that were severe enough to freeze the shingle into concrete and have yet to suffer from cold. A wind-break, such as a fisherman's large umbrella, is also a good investment.

The second essential is to gather your own bait. Lugworm is the most effective of all baits and is often in short supply during the winter months. Demand is very high, and the weather and tides frequently prevent diggers from gathering enough to fill their order-books. By digging your own, you guarantee your supply and you ensure that you have first-class baits when the fish are around to take them.

The third essential is casting skill. Cod—especially large ones—are often reluctant to move close in to shore. Nobody is quite sure why this should be. However, as in many fishing situations, anglers come to realize that they often know more about fishing than they understand. Whatever the reason, high-velocity, long-range casting is probably the single factor which gives some anglers big bags while those around are scratching for stragglers. It is highly satisfying to be the only angler on the beach to catch any cod at all. However, you can reach this position only after suffering the frustrations and enduring the boredom of long hours of practice. The activity is rather like riding a bicycle. Once the technique is learnt, it is never lost. A few short sessions each autumn soon polish skills back into form.

Only time, dedication and tuition will teach you the powerful techniques that have been proven on the tournament field to be capable of propelling baits out to the motorways along which feeding bands of fish will be travelling. The results of such practice can be measured in greatly improved catches. Because cod are so prolific, and such good sport can be had simply by observing a handful of basic points, it is sheer folly not to take the small amount of trouble that will instantly put you into the big-bag league.

Cod, like most sea fish, move about according to the abundance of food. They are interested only in filling their stomach with a minimum of effort. During the winter months they seem to have three main sources of food—sprats, which form into huge shoals during the cold months; small whiting, pouting and other fish that are often abundant inshore during this season; and the spoils of a deep depression which, with winds of force 10 and higher, creates massive waves which plough up the sea bed and expose masses of worms and shellfish, which would otherwise be hidden from the cods' attention. Unfortunately there seems to be little the angler can do when the fish are attacking sprats. Sometimes, when the shoals of silvery tiddlers come close to shore, they are washed up. Very rarely do sprats works as bait, because the cod are grabbing live fish some way up from the sea-bed. Live sprats rarely survive being hooked and cast out. However, big fish which are foraging after a storm will take them from time to time. However, such fish are usually full

Night tide on a top cod beach.

of a wide variety of food items, ranging from crabs to sea mice, lugworms, razor fish and so on. One cod that was brought ashore on a sprat, weighed 26 lb (11.5 kg) even after disgorging a silver eel.

When the sea is calm and few sprat shoals are around to distract them, the cod will feed heartily on small fish. The trick here is simple, but requires a certain amount of patience and confidence for success. Make up a two-hook tackle. Tie a 5/0 to the end of your trace, then fix a length of nylon just above the bend of this hook, on the shank, with a spade-end knot. Tie a 1/0 so that it hangs some 3 in (7.5 cm) away from the big hook.

Some anglers bait only the small hook, threading on a single lugworm so that one end lies over the small hook's barb, while the other end is tight against the big hook. It will not be long, if plenty of tiddlers are out there, before the rod-tip is jiggling about, signifying that one has swallowed the small hook. It is now effectively tethered close to a hook that is large enough to hold onto a big cod. A passing cod will sense its distress and home in on the victim. Sometimes you may have to wait an hour before the rod suddenly bends as a hefty fish strikes the baitfish. Occasionally it will happen within a minute. Double-figure fish are usually the ones caught by this technique, though sometimes a mere 6 lb (2.7 kg) fish will grab hold.

Another variation is to bait both hooks. Two large lugworms are folded, then tied to the big hook with elastic thread. Even if the whiting manages to escape with the worm, or gets free, the other bait is still there to attract a cod. Sometimes a very large cod will like the idea of such a massive bait and will swallow it all.

Casting skill is a basic essential for the cod fisherman.

A brace of 14-pounders (6.5 kg) from Dungeness.

The trick is effective in those seasons when few run-of-the-mill fish are about, and opportunities come from just one or two small groups of large fish that wander down the beach during the tide. While 6–7 in (15–18 cm) whiting seem to be most attractive, I have caught fish that have taken whiting weighing in the region of 2 lb (900 g). Rockling, dabs and small soles also work on such a rig.

The fishing can be excellent after a heavy storm has passed through and excavated the beach. However, much depends on the nature of your particular beach. Shallow east coast beaches tend to fish poorly for several days after a very big gale. The fish can be unsettled by a deep depression, even on beaches that boast a fair depth of water close in. You must judge how big the seas should be before they benefit the beaches you fish, and discover when conditions are so severe that they wipe out sport for a few days.

However, the nett result is about the same. Masses of worms and shellfish are unearthed by the breakers. Cod feed on them as they drift around just offshore. However, if strong currents are running when the storm is at its height, there is a fair chance that all this feed will follow the tide offshore and take the fish with it. Then again, there have been times when this feed has been washed back inshore several days later, and huge catches have been made. The tideline is a good guide. Your chances should be good when worms, sea-mice and shellfish are washing ashore. However, as with all fishing, hard-and-fast rules are impossible to make. You have to play your own hunches.

Baits for cod are legion. It has been said that this species will eat anything that does not attack it first. However, lugworm is the beach-fisherman's staple. Very often cocktails prove to be more effective. Once a group of friends brought clams from Wales to Dungeness. The white, meaty syphons outfished even freshly-dug black lugworms. Razor-fish, mussels, slipper limpets and whelk guts have all worked well in cocktails with lugworm. Soft baits should be tied to the hook with elastic thread, the lugworms acting as splints.

Because these fish are feeding by scent, juicy worms are effective. Lugworms should not be gutted—not even large black ones—for fear of losing valuable natural groundbait. A general rule that applies to all species is: change the bait if you are not catching fish while those around you are. The juices may have been washed out, destroying its appeal. This assumes that you have confidence in your tackle, and your casting is good.

Tackle for cod consists of a fine-tipped casting rod and reel, many anglers use a matched pair, and 10 lb (4.50 kg) line for open-beach codding. They make sure that their leaders are strong enough to take the shock of the cast and that all knots are cleanly tied. And they check their lines for abrasion and damage after each session. Terminal rigs are streamlined so as to reduce air resistance on the cast and sinkers are generally wired bombs which tether the bait in one spot on the sea-bed. There is little point in putting out an attractively-scented bait if it is going to drift about, thus reducing the effectiveness of its scent-trail.

The extent of the winter cod season varies from place to place around our coastline. However, in some places, such as the south-east corner of Kent, there is a run of fish in spring. They come into rocky, reefy areas hunting for crabs. Canny anglers import peeler crabs from the coast of Devon, paying a high price for each one, and have good success using tactics and tackle that are very similar to those employed against reef bass in high summer.

These fish can be quite aggressive when hooked. I recall a period many years ago when the winter cod run seemed to last for ever. The fish showed no inclination to move away from the shoreline, even though the winter was quite severe. They would appear at virtually every location where I chose to fish. I eventually settled for a small local pier—a sewer pipe—and caught plenty of 3–5 lb (1.3–2.2 kg) fish on peeler crabs that I had gathered in a backwater of a local estuary. The water there had warmed up sufficiently to encourage a few crabs to shed their shells. The fish were as lazy as usual when hooked, but would dive with great power and doggedness when I tried to raise them up in the water for netting. On several occasions the tip-ring of my light bass rod would be dragged under water. Such sport sticks in the mind.

Winter codding from piers is popular with some people, though not with this writer. The exposed vantage points require close attention to insulation. Tactics can be the same as those used off the beach, though a drop-net or a drop-gaff is essential to land the really big fish. There is an art in drop-netting, so accept assistance only from people you can trust. Once I was fishing a pier during rough weather that blotted out local beaches. Another angler hooked a monster cod. His buddy went to net it and, because it was so rough, wound the line round his hands, taking several turns round his thumb for good measure. His intention was to control the fish as it wallowed 10 ft (3 m) below him. A freak wave appeared, a travelling mound of white water. It caught the cod with great force, and the line was dragged up so tight that it cleanly cut off the top joint of the netsman's thumb. A salutary lesson indeed.

Besides following reports of cod catches and exploiting your intelligence system in other ways, it pays to keep an ear open for the catches of boat anglers. Once I learnt that the boats were doing very well close into a massive reef, just half a mile from land. One night, when I had bait left over after a disappointing session from an open beach, I decided to try fishing from the rocks, casting out to a patch of sand with just 5–6 ft (1.5–1.8 m) of water over it. I took only one fish that session. It weighed 14 lb (6.3 kg). Next time I went, my score was better, but the highlight of the trip was a 7 lb (3.1 kg) bass. Several such fish are caught in November from cod beaches, normally in the shallower, more surfy water, after a storm has gouged out plenty of bait.

These bass, I have always assumed, are migrating to their over-wintering zones. However, as the sea is still quite warm early in the winter, there is no reason why they should not be feeding. Naturally I was elated by my January 7 lb (3.1 kg) fish, but I later learnt that it was no freak. Some anglers catch even larger ones from sand and reef areas during the winter months. More anglers should turn their attention that way because it appears that success is there and waiting to be grasped. Warm weather is vital for success. The bass will not tolerate cruel temperatures, even though the cod may linger there a little longer.

This type of rock fishing is pure joy compared to the rugged rough-bottom fishing around the Yorkshire area. There the anglers use line as thick as hawsers for the cod. They, too, have their seasonal migrations of very large fish. It must be very frustrating to hang into a hefty cod from such a rock mark and to feel it go solid in rubbery kelp. It is not unknown for anglers to cut their line, tie the seaward end to a rock, and attempt to regain the fish at low tide. Tackle and tactics for rough-bottom Yorkshire fishing are essentially very similar to those used by reef bass anglers, except that the tackle is stepped-up in power. Poker-like rods and reels like winches (with the Scarborough centre-pin ideal for this purpose) are employed to good effect.

These folk also fish off the tops of cliffs and other vantage points where it is impossible to get near the sea. They suffer horribly when they hook into large cod, because the hook is likely to tear out of the fish's mouth under pressure from its dead-weight.

Cod have soft mouths, which is why you will never see an experienced open-beach fishermen try to horse them in too fast. This species is commonly lost by tyros who become over-excited at hooking something big and who are over-anxious to get a look at the fish. The best method of playing a fish is to wind down until the rod is moderately bent and let this bend—or, rather, the spring of it—ease the cod shorewards. As the rod straightens, the angler reels in more line so as to maintain a consistent, telling pressure on the fish. However, as cod anglers know, cod often swim to shore and it is possible to reel in as though nothing is on the end. However, the fish is likely to wake up when it feels the surf or senses that the bottom is shallowing. Then is the time to keep the rod-tip high and bent.

Provided that the reel's drag mechanism is adjusted so that the fish can take line when the bend in the rod becomes too severe, there is little chance of a fish escaping. If it becomes embroiled in surf, the fish can take line without the wave-pressure tearing it off the hook or, worse, breaking free.

Many anglers are scaling down their tackle for cod

Big cod demand generous helpings of bait.

fishing, with light line becoming more widely used. However, it is the winter flounder fisherman who is likely to have the biggest surprises.

Early in the New Year many anglers change to light tackle for the flounders which move down estuaries to the open sea prior to spawning off-shore. A storm at such a time is likely to uncover masses of shellfish which these flatties gobble up with great glee. However, stray cod are also attracted by such bonanzas and I can well remember catching a series of 7–8 lb (3–3.6 kg) fish one day while using a light spinning rod and 7 lb (3 kg) line for flounders. I failed to catch any flatties at all, but had great fun fighting these cod through substantial surf. The realization that the fish had less time for fighting than I had helped me to take things easily. This is logical, of course, though it is easily forgotten in the heat of the moment. Provided that the hook is still in the fish, you have all the time in the world to think about landing it.

Some cod anglers also go for the dabs which abound inshore in winter. They fix a size 6 hook to the lead clip with a short length of line and, because dabs are not too hot on heaving 6 oz (180 g) grapnel leads over the ocean shore, leave the tackle out there until a cod takes the main bait.

Sometimes a whiting takes this small hook. This is a bad thing because a 30 lb (13.5 kg) cod is likely to come along and grab the whiting, and would not get hooked. However, dabs tend to feed much closer to the shoreline than cod. On most beaches the inshore run is to be found where the shingle meets the sand. Yes, the biggest dabs are caught from boats, but that is a different environment altogether. Catches of either species are likely to be higher if they are approached in a single-minded manner, perhaps by fishing two rods at a time, with one directed at the dabs, the other at the cod.

There is one tiddler that can be hooked by the cod fisherman who goes armed with 5/0 hooks baited with lugworm: sole. These fish are not deterred by heavy hooks, they simply eat their way around the bend of the hook, impaling themselves in the process. Some specimen soles are caught by cod anglers. However, this is not as much fun as catching them on a muggy night in July.

Boat fishing

SPRING: WRECKING

Two world wars, erratic navigation and primitive weather forecasting over the last hundred years have conspired to litter the sea-bed with wrecks of ships. Look at any chart for the sea areas between England and Europe—and others—and you will see that the sea floor is liberally littered with wrecks. Marine sports-men are an optimistic bunch. Instead of viewing all these structures in terms of the immeasurable amount of human suffering each must have caused, not to mention the loss of property and headaches for insurance men, fishermen regard them as holding areas for good fish.

Huge cod and larger pollack often form dense shoals over wrecks, especially those that have not been dynamited to make a clear path for more fortunate ships. On the echo-sounder, these shoals show up as dense clouds above the steepling black line of the wreck like bats round the spires of Dracula's castle.

A cod being brought to the boat. Hooks must be very strong as cod hit pirks with fierce determination.

Respect the sea—and your insurance policy.

These fish are there to feed, taking herrings, sprats, launce, mackerel and capelin which come to them on the tide. And plenty of small species like red bream and pouting also inhabit such territory.

Each spring sees some enormous hauls of fish being taken from wrecks. The largest that I have heard of totalled 3 tons of cod, pollack and ling in one tide between eight anglers. How their backs and shoulders must have ached next day. At times they must have felt as though their arms were about to drop off.

Wreck fishing cannot be called a sporting exercise. It is meat fishing at its most raw. Pollack, ling, cod, coalfish and even little red bream soon become puffed out when the water pressure decreases while they are being brought to the boat. Ling suffer very badly. Their eyes go like golf-balls and their swim bladder protrudes from their mouth. Not the best condition in which to put up a heroic struggle. If the water is not too deep, coalfish and cod suffer less.

Most wrecking trips are made on board a charter boat that is owned by a skipper who knows the grounds and, more important, knows which wrecks the fish prefer to gang up over. One wreck may fish well for a day or two, but the fish tend to move about.

Obviously a fast boat is an advantage because it allows you to move from wreck to wreck very quickly until a sizeable blip of fish shows on the echo-sounder. However, most charter boats can only make a handful of knots even when running flat out, so most trips start with a lengthy haul out to the grounds. And a long run back. As most charter skippers work no more than a ten hour day, there is ample time between these long runs for the anglers to grow weary of hauling up fish that barely fight.

However, if you are fit and can afford tanks of fuel, a professional-grade echo-sounder and a Decca navigation rig, large hauls could be made over a period of time. However, few skippers are likely to let slip the location of good wrecks, and they even note them down with reference numbers that are not true to the correct Decca bearing.

Many anglers go wrecking with just an echo-sounder, relying on shore bearings to locate structures that lie relatively close to land. The problem is that their outboard-powered 18 ft (5.5 m) planing hulls do not come up out of the water when laden with ½ ton of fish; the boat sits so low in the water that one rogue wave could roll it.

Most anglers go wrecking with a charter skipper. His knowledge of where to find fish is vital to success. He is, after all, out there nearly every day when the weather smiles. His familiarity with the structures enables him to select which part of a wreck to fish over, and then to tell his anglers when to wind like hell so that their lures do not snag into the superstructure. He also knows which wrecks are draped with nets from trammel netsmen and ambitious trawlers, and can avoid such snaggy parts.

Except when fishing for congers, wrecks are fished on the drift. Thus the anglers can work their lures around the structure and the boat's movement imparts life to their pirks, feathers and similar hardware. Some wrecks lie in very deep water. Because nylon line stretches and rods flex, it becomes almost impossible to work a pirk at such depths. Many anglers prefer to fish deep-water wrecks when a swell is running. This will raise and lower the boat, imparting movement to the pirks. Under calm conditions, the hardware barely twitches. Wire line would obviate this, but few wreck fishermen use it. It would work well provided that a nylon leader is fixed between the reel line and the lures. This should be lighter in strength than the main line so that it breaks more readily if snagged. Braided line is thick and because it tangles badly with nylon, few anglers use it, even though it does not stretch much. However, a nylon leader is also recommended here to take the abrasion of the structure which would fray and severely damage the braid.

Big wreck cod demand large pirks, feathers, plastic squids—or any kind of junk that can be fitted with a hook and fished right.

A handsome ling. These fish respond well to baited pirk.

A fairly stiff rod is recommended for maximum movement of lures. Carbon fibre is a useful material here, and blanks are available with little flex in them some 3 ft (90 cm) back from the tip. Thus the backbone of the rod is strong enough to work the lures while the tip is adequate for playing fish. Lines of 20 lb (9 kg) are fine for wrecks lying in twenty fathoms of water, with 30 lb (14 kg) suitable for greater depths. When fishing for pollack and coalfish, different techniques are employed, so I should point out here that I am talking about general pirking tactics. When meat fishing with multi-hooked traces over well-stocked wrecks, heavier line is needed to haul three 25 lb (11.3 kg) fish aboard at a time. This approach does not appeal to everybody, however.

A reel with high gearing is not suitable for wrecking. I use Ambassadeur 9000 reels because they change to a lower gear when the pressure is on, thus making hauling less hard work. It is vital that the angler understands how to pump fish aboard by hauling the rod up high, lifting the fish in the water, then winding in line while dropping the tip to horizontal.

Many wrecking situations call for pirks. These can be bought at fancy prices which rise to around £8.00 a time. Because they can be lost so easily when snagged, most anglers make their own from pipe. This is hammered flat at one end and bent at an angle so that the water catches this area and causes the beast to wobble. The rest of the pipe is filled with lead. Different gauge tubes make for different sizes and weights of lure. Pirks can be chromed or covered with reflective prismatic tape. Some of the most effective are simply sprayed yellow. A huge treble hook is fixed to one end by a piece of wire that is moulded into the lead when the thing is created. A hole in the flat flange at the other end will take a stout clip for fixing to the bitter end of the line.

If you use split-rings and similar clips, make sure they are strong. A hefty cod can shake his head a few times and snap weak ones. Hooks must be strong because cod hit pirks with fierce determination. Cod have a huge mouth, and the hook has to be large to catch in it. Once, when bassing with pirks, I kept experiencing a succession of bumps at the pirk, then nothing. Eventually one such series led to the boating of a cod, and I realized that the treble was not getting a chance to hook in anywhere. I changed to bigger pirks and caught more cod, fewer bass.

Other hardware is used for wrecking. Size 6/0 O'Shaughnessy hooks fastooned with a skirt made from a black dustbin bag can work wonders. If you fancy a different colour, like yellow, tie strips of yellow fertilizer sack onto the hook. Now you know what to do with your old Gro-bags at summer's end. Such lures are large and appeal to cod. Commercial cod feathers and similar confections are generally too small.

All you do is drop the tackle overboard when the skipper tells you to and, when the boat comes to a rest, let the spool go until you tap bottom. Cod and ling live close to the sea-bed, so wind in 1–2 yd (1–2 m) and start jigging. If, after a couple of drifts, nothing has taken, the skipper may move to another wreck. If he does not move on after half a dozen blank drifts, cross that skipper out of your address book. If cod are there, they will take almost immediately.

Even pirks should be fitted with sharp hooks, so there is little point in striking if you experience a hefty take. That fish will have hooked itself. If you are using multiple lures, you may have to haul a dead weight of three or four fish from maybe forty fathoms. Multi-lure traces, incidentally, should be made up on 100 lb (45 kg) nylon or there will be breakages.

Ling often prefer to find a chunk of bait on the pirk's treble before they will attack it. They are attracted by scent and vibration, as well as sight, assuming that light penetrates to the depth at which your outfit is fishing.

Many anglers take a few bags of frozen mackerel with them so as not to waste time fishing for them while over a wreck. This normally proves to be adequate. Mackerel should be frozen very fresh if they are to be of any use as bait. Even then they tend to fall apart once thawed out. However, as only a little scent is necessary, a half-side fixed at one end to one of the treble hooks is sufficient to interest ling.

Pollack and coalfish also take pirks. However, these two species are not so often found feeding on the sea bed. Instead they will often be above the wreck or hovering close to the down-tide edge. Sadly, wreck pollack are unable to cope with rapid decompression when hauled up from any great depth of water. Even when 6–12 lb (2.70–5.50 kg) class tackle is used, their initial dive is often absorbed by the line so that the angler feels himself pulling in a dead weight which, when it comes close to the boat, streams bubbles from its gills when its swim-bladder ruptures. Many anglers who fish purely for sport prefer to chase pollack over more shallow grounds, such as reefs that lie in only a few fathoms of water. They may not grow so large, but they put up a more spirited fight.

Although many pollack are caught on pirks and feathers being fished close to the sea-bed for cod and ling, pollack are more likely to come to a redgill eel fished on a long trace. Just one is used, with the trace tied to a boom that was specially developed for this work. The boom is L-shaped. The long part is about 1 ft 6 in (45 cm) in length, the shorter part about 6 in (15 cm). The sinker is clipped to an eye in the corner of the 'L'; the line is attached to the short part and the trace to the longer part. Thus the redgill can be dropped down without swinging up and tangling with the main line. Redgills—and similar lures—are fished thus. When the sinker hits bottom, start retrieving line, but not too fast. Some days the pollack—and coalfish—like the lure to move fast; on other days it should creep up in the water. The idea is that the little fish swims straight through the pollack shoals hovering over the structure. Several taps may be experienced before a fish grabs hold and dives. Red and black have proved to be very effective colours, although other colours also score.

The tackle should be wound all the way back to the boat because sometimes both pollack and coalfish stalk it and take at the last moment. This tactic covers a great depth of water, which is essential for coalfish, because they feed at different levels at any time of the day. Wreck pollack, like their reef-dwelling cousins, leave the structure at dusk and swim high in the water, sometimes close to the surface where they can be caught on spinning rods. As they are bound to be large fish, sport is guaranteed to be hectic and immense fun. They will have decompressed themselves gradually on the way up and will fight with full fury.

A tactic that sometimes pays off for both these species is to use a pirk and tap bottom, then reel it to the surface at great speed. The action entices shy coalfish, which will hit the rod very hard. However, if the fish are scarce, the tactic can be quite tiring on the angler.

Coalfish are magnificent beasts, almost salmon-shaped. They are very powerful and dogged fighters. They are also great roamers, so catches cannot be guaranteed from one day to the next. Best results from large coalies come early in the New Year up to springtime when the fish come to spawn over wrecks. Pollack also gang up to spawn at this time and very large hauls of big fish are made, although some anglers have doubts about the ethics of hammering fish which are intent on starting off future generations.

The peak of the wreck cod season varies around Britain. Very large fish—30 lb (14 kg) and more—are taken from wrecks at the eastern end of the English Channel from April onwards. Off Whitby, the best begins a little later and peaks in mid-summer, a time when many southern skippers are having to work harder for their fish.

Ling are available all through the year. Wrecks are an almost permanent home for them, though again the largest fish are taken when full of spawn early in the year. The largest specimens come from the West Country.

Much ill-will has been experienced between anglers and skippers in the past over the question of how much of the catch can be taken off the boat, and how much reverts to the skipper. This is no easy question. Skippering a wreck boat is not a good way to earn money. However, a group of anglers who might charter a top skipper for a fortnight and who sell all they catch may well earn more per day than the skipper makes each week if the fishing is good.

Discussion on this subject should take place at the time of booking the boat, so that if you do not like the

The common feather proves irresistible to pollack.

skipper's rules you can find another one. However, it is customary in big-game centres around the world to tip the boat's mate—the man who does all the work. In the UK, where finances are more slender and the skipper is also the mate for much of the time, it is a courtesy to leave about half of a really big haul on board for the skipper—or, if the fishing has not been so good, just a few fish.

The skipper's goodwill is more important than the bare finances and divisions of the catch. Unless you are a once-a-year wreck fisherman, it pays to cultivate a sound friendship with good skippers. They then feel obliged to put good fishing your way, and you are obliged to fish hard and catch them. Likewise, it pays to drop out from parties that acquire a bad reputation in a port. Word gets around and your presence on board a boat will be tolerated only because you are paying. This is a very bad state of affairs. At the other end of the scale, you could get a telephone call late one night: 'Be down at the harbour at 8.00. We took 3000 lb today, seventeen cod over 30 lb. I've got no party booked for tomorrow, so we'll make it a meat-fishing trip.'

There are other species of fish to be found around wrecks. The conger is just one, and is dealt with in a later chapter. Turbot are also found around some wrecks. These are generally large specimens. Tactics for them are the same as those employed for most general bottom fishing: half a mackerel hooked at the thin end so that the tide catches the thick end and wafts it about enticingly. Use a quite long trace for this, about 6 ft (1.8 m) long, and a boom to prevent the bait from swinging up and tangling with the line.

Turbot should be given plenty of time to take baits properly. They are delicious table-fare, so every opportunity should be taken to ensure that the transfer from seabed to fish box goes without a hitch. When a turbot takes, set the hook but do not exert too much pressure. They have large mouths, much of which is thin membrane that can easily tear. Fortunately turbot don't fight much, though occasionally one takes a dislike to the boat and makes a half-hearted dive. When fishing in deep water, the hook-hold is likely to have enlarged into a hole during the hauling process. It is essential that a tight line is kept at the boatside, and that the fish is not lifted too close to the surface where it can thrash around and possibly throw the hook. If the line is allowed to go slack, the hook can just fall out.

Another species which is common around wrecks, especially those in the West Country and Off Ireland, is the red bream. These are often ignored by anglers who pursue the larger species of fish that inhabit these structures. However, red bream are handsome fish, plucky fighters and very tasty when baked with a few herbs. They are, of course, essentially reef fish, which like other wreck-dwellers, cannot differentiate between a rusting hull and a pinnacle of granite. Many anglers go for red bream when they are to be found on shallow-water reefs. However, some wreck fishermen, especially those who have lost the fanatic urge to haul big fish all day long, like to have a crack at the bream by way of light relief.

Scaled-down tackle is essential for these fish: 6–12 lb (2.70–5.50 kg) class boat rods and small multipliers. A longish trace is used, with a boom to prevent the bait swinging up and tangling the line when the tackle is lowered to the sea-bed. A 1/0 hook is ample, loaded with the silvery half of a side of mackerel. This is nicked onto the hook a couple of times at one end so that the bait can move seductively. After tapping bottom—if the bait gets that far—reel in a few turns so that the boat's movement causes the mackerel strip to waft about down there. Bites are usually a heavy rattle followed by a good pull. The hooked fish is guaranteed to give a good account of itself. And it will give you cause to reflect that fish do not have to be huge for the catching of them to be fun.

SUMMER: SHARKS

Sharks are the health-care officials of the sea: anything in trouble gets the chop. This ancient group of species is famous for the razor-sharp teeth that put a swift end to the sick, the injured, and those unable to escape fast enough. Nature has equipped them magnificently for this task. They detect prey through water-borne vibrations, through a sense of smell that can pick out the weakest imaginable dilutions of blood, and through receiving electrical impulses emitted by the nervous system of hidden fish. Some sharks also have very efficient eye-sight.

There are some thirty-two species to be found around the British Isles. Some live at depths that defy deep-sea angling. Others are very rare. British anglers are familiar with smaller species such as the lesser spotted dogfish, the bull huss, the two smooth-hounds, and the spur-dog. The larger sharks include the monkfish, the tope, the thresher, the porbeagle, the mako and the blue.

The basking shark is one of the largest sharks there is, but it feeds exclusively on plankton. The fisherman who works out how to mount krill in an appealing manner on to a size 10/0 Seamaster hook is likely to make a name for himself. Another monster, the Greenland shark, prefers depths greater than 100 fathoms and very cold water. It feasts on puffins, penguins, seals, cod and skate and grows to a great

A handsome blue shark that has been brought to the boat.

age. As a sporting proposition, however, the fish is a dead loss. Its generic name, *Somniosus*, means 'sleepy'. It allows itself to be hauled into the boat without putting up any fight at all.

One of the rarest sharks of all round the British Isles is the mako. This tough angling proposition is an oceanic shark, preferring to stay away from the coastline. It is occasionally caught where the Atlantic washes our islands with clear, blue water. Cornwall and southern Ireland are likely spots. However, it spends more time tracking the off-shore migrations of

cod, capelin and albacore, so it is unlikely to become too interested in a pair of dead mackerel lying in a rubby-dubby slick. However, about once a year one becomes too curious and is hooked. These huge game sharks grow to over ½ ton in weight and fight with rare verve. They are among the sea's most powerful and dogged fighters; more are lost than are boated.

This chapter will concern itself with the likely propositions that are worth spending money and effort in catching. These include the thresher, porbeagle, and blue sharks, tope and monkfish.

The monkfish is the largest of a group of bottom-dwelling sharks that is represented throughout the world's seas. Some species are smothered with fringes and similar fleshy growths, which disguise them on the sea bed where they lie in ambush for small fish and

115

molluscs. The British monkfish looks rather like a cross between a ray and a shark. Its sporting characteristics are slight. However, some mariners have discovered that the way to get a fight out of a monkfish is to prod it with a gaff until it becomes irate. This species is found in fairly localized areas—large shallow bays—where consistent catches can be made. Outsize specimens appear to be loners. Tralee Bay in Ireland is one of the best-known areas for good monk-fishing. The fish has one characteristic that should be guarded against. It feeds by lunging at anything that is incautious enough to come within range of its jaws. When boated, it is liable to lunge at an unwary hand or foot.

Other sharks are much better sporting propositions. Tope are fairly abundant round the British Isles. In some places they can be caught from the open beach and from rock marks, but boat fishing gives the most consistent sport. Best fishing is in shallow water—20 ft (6 m) or less—with male fish. These are characterized by the pair of claspers close to the anus, a feature that distinguishes all sharks and rays as male. They do not grow as big as females, but group together into packs. When hooked on light tackle, these fish will run well and sometimes leap. Females are more sedate when hooked, except in very shallow water where they tear off at great speed. They tend to be dour and dogged in water over six fathoms in depth. They average out at around 35–50 lb (15–22 kg) each, however, unlike the males which average 15–25 lb (6–11 kg).

Tope feed over all types of sea-bed, from pinnacle rock to flat sand. They are relatively omnivorous in that all species of small fish from bass to mackerel appeal to them, as well as crabs, squids and cuttlefish. There are many recognized tope areas in Britain where consistent catches can be made. However, while peak season along the south coast is June and July, the best fishing in Scotland's Luce Bay is in September. These fish are great wanderers, and tagged specimens have been recaptured (after tagging in English waters) from the Canary Islands, the Mediterranean, the Bay of Biscay, and so on.

A related species is the blue shark. This is another oceanic species which does not like to come too close to land where salinity is lowered by rivers debouching into the sea. These sharks are found exclusively round the southern and western coasts of England and Ireland. Because the British Isles marks one of the northerly limits of their range, blues are very sensitive to water temperature. They feed best when hot calm spells have heated up the surface water. However, the water in our latitudes appears never to be warm enough to make them fight hard and specimens hooked out from Cornish ports do not put up half the battle of blues taken off sub-tropical coasts.

Unfortunately blues encourage the worst possible form of sharking. This is practised out of some Cornish tourist ports. The sport has an aura of danger which films like *Jaws* have done nothing to dispel from the public imagination. However, the sharks off Looe are tiddler blues, of tope-like proportions, with perhaps one 100 lb (45 kg) fish among every hundred hooked. Because the public are encouraged to believe that they are likely to hook into something huge, very powerful tackle is hired out to the tourists. Besides, such tackle looks very macho in the holiday snaps which will be handed round the pub a fortnight or so later. And, of course, the massive reels and Herculean lines do not get anything like the wear they were built to withstand so the skippers have little maintenance to do on them. Some anglers have caught blues on very skinny tackle and have had great fun in doing so, even though such tackle would be more at home on a pike lake.

One shark that does give a good run-around is the thresher. Some skippers believe that this fish is more common than is generally believed because it feeds on the bottom for much of its life, devouring dabs and pouting from sand and rock marks close to shore. However, it also eats mackerel and pilchards, using its tail like a flail to terrify the bait-fish into compact balls through which it charges with its mouth gaping, returning afterwards to mop up the injured. This fish is instantly identified by this huge tail.

In some years, there is an abundance of thresher pups inshore. Boat anglers see them leaping, or may hook into them while tope fishing. Newhaven pier, in Sussex, used to attract these 50 lb (22 kg) fish because large shoals of mackerel used to linger there for much of the summer, and the estuary was full of mullet, school bass and flatfish for variety of diet. Such occurrences are rare nowadays. Occasionally one of these pups would be hooked by somebody who had come to fish for mackerel or flounders. He would find that a hooked mackerel had been taken by a thresher pup that would rush off at top speed before destroying the line, leaving the unsuspecting angler thoroughly shaken and wondering what had hit him.

The star of UK shark fishing has to be the porbeagle shark. This fellow loves offshore reefs and tends to shun clear ground. It feeds largely by sight, as is obvious from its huge eyes, and tends to prefer live baits to dead ones. It also is the only British shark that can regularly be caught by trolling: dragging a bait behind a moving boat.

This species is fairly abundant round the UK. Many rocky sites are well-known as porgie feeding grounds, and most are close to shore. Some have even been hooked and landed from favoured Irish rocky shores.

Other sites, like wrecks, are often ignored because the anglers prefer to fish for edible cod and pollack rather than inedible sharks. Several porgies are hooked each year out from Newhaven, well away from land, by wreck fishermen. Because interest is so slight, the potential has not been explored. Porgies eat anything from wrasse to mackerel, though they do not appear to be too interested in bottom-dwellers, such as flat-fish.

Boat anglers should fish light for sharks, encouraging them to run and tire themselves out rather than just hauling them into the boat, which is exhausting for the angler. Boat rod tips of 6, 12 and 20 lb (2.70, 5.50 and 9 kg) classes are ideal for all tope situations. Class outfits of 20–50 lb (9–23 kg) are suitable for threshers and porbeagles, while the indolent blue shark performs best on 12–30 lb (5.50–14 kg) line. Ian Bunney of Leicester has taken porbeagles on 6 and 12 lb (2.60 and 5.50 kg) class outfits, but as he has been fishing with this sort of light tackle for many years, he has the skill not to snap out of hooked fish. However, many anglers consider this ultra-light fishing to be somewhat irresponsible because several sharks are likely to be lost, and these will escape trailing a long trace which could tangle with the sea-bed and anchor the fish so that it drowns.

Enormous reels are not necessary. For porbeagle, 400 yd (400 m) of line will prove to be ample. Tope can be tackled with medium-sized beach-casting multipliers. What is important, however, is that rod, reel

An average male tope comes aboard, off Eastbourne. Few anglers kill these fighters nowadays—most are put back.

and line must be balanced—there is no advantage to be gained from fishing 50 lb (23 kg) line on a 30 lb (14 kg) rod. Knots must be perfect and traces carefully built.

In order to preserve maximum line strength, tie a clip to the end of the main line with a Bimini jamb. This is formed by passing the line twice through the clip, then twisting it back on itself for ½ in (12 mm) in open turns. Now whip the line in close, touching turns back towards the clip. Instead of a final turn, make a half-hitch round the open turns, followed by another two round the clip. This attachment is 100 per cent strong and is used throughout the world's game fish centres for line-class fishing for marlin, sailfish and tuna—fish that fight back.

The trace is made up to about 15–20 ft (4.5–6 m) long for big sharks, less for tope. Because their skin is smothered in denticles—tiny teeth—any thin line that touches their hide is liable to be abraded and will snap. Shark anglers use commercial nylon of about 200 lb (90 kg) test for the rubbing leader. This is crimped instead of knotted, using crimps normally employed for making wire traces. A swivel is fixed at each end—one for the clip that terminates the main line, the other for the steel trace which has to cope with those fearsome teeth. Swivels for shark fishing should be very large, not to withstand the strain of a fish, but to provide a grip on the leader when the fish is hauled to the boat for gaffing or release. Some anglers mount a third swivel mid-way along the nylon trace.

The steel trace is crimped to one swivel. Bowden cable—as used for motorbike brakes—makes suitable trace wire and is virtually impregnable to shark teeth. Lighter wire can be used for blue sharks and tope because they do not shake their heads at boatside as

much as threshers and porbeagle. This shaking causes the fish's teeth to saw at the trace and will sever light wire. Even so, fish like tope can bite through 40 lb (18 kg) trace wire, so 100 lb (45 kg) is more reliable. An 80 lb (36 kg) rubbing leader, about 8–10 ft (2.5–3 m) long, is adequate for tope. It is also adequate for small blues, but this species tends to roll itself up in the trace, so should be very much longer to allow for this.

Size 6/0 O'Shaughnessy hooks are adequate for tope and small blues, with 10/0 and 12/0 Mustad Seamasters more popular for the bigger sharks because they require larger baits. All hooks should be of carbon steel if fish are to be released. Thus a well-hooked fish can be liberated simply by cutting the wire trace. The fish is well able to get rid of the hook itself and even a deep-seated one will disintegrate very quickly. This is preferable to the all-out wresting match that ensues when a shark is brought aboard for removal of the hooks. This activity is likely to be the shark's last because it causes internal organs to rupture and the fish ultimately dies even if it survives the surgery of a boat-man and an angler.

Stainless steel O'Shaughnessy hooks can be used for tope when they are not swallowing hooks deep down. Under these circumstances, where the hook is easily reached, grab it in a pair of pliers and the fish's thrashing will snap the more brittle hook.

Traces can be rigged specifically for releasing sharks. Instead of fixing the hook to the trace in the normal manner, poke the wire through the hook eye and form a loop round which the hook can swing. The crimp is placed about 10 in (25 cm) away from the hook so that the boatman need only cut through one side of this loop for the wire to slide free and release the fish unharmed. Only 3 ft (90 cm) of steel is required for sharks, half that needed for tope. Never use nylon-covered wire because the covering will be torn to tatters and wear can be concentrated into one small area.

Blood attracts sharks quicker than anything else. Most shark trips start out with a mackerel-fishing session. A box holding 5 st (32 kg) of mackerel will provide both bait and the raw material for rubby-dubby. Some anglers have trouble catching mackerel. The secret is to discover the depth at which they are feeding. Start jigging just under the boat, but with the reel out of gear and a thumb holding the spool. After about ten jigs, pay out another 6 ft (1.8 m) of line and continue the process until you tap bottom. Work out how far down the fish are by how much line you have paid out. Mackerel rarely feed on the bottom and are usually to be found between 10 and 30 ft (3–9 m) beneath the surface.

It is not always necessary to fill up a box with mackerel before starting to fish for sharks. Rubby-dubby attracts them, too, and once when I was sharking on the Irish sea, the boat seemed to be drifting among a sea of mackerel. Shoals of them kept welling up at the boatside. I bet the skipper £1 that he could not touch bottom in half an hour using a 6 oz (180 g) sinker and five mackerel feathers. He gave up trying in the end. Every time he threw his tackle overboard, he let the reel run, but the mackerel stopped it before it had gone 20 ft (6 m) and he had to haul in another stringful.

Rubby-dubby is essential to success. This is made up from chopped up mackerel mixed with dried blood, fish oil and bran to bulk it out. The mackerel are processed by slicing them crossways with a bread knife. The sharp, serrated edges to this utensil does the job quickly and without undue strain on the wrist. After thirty mackerel have been sliced as thinly as possible, they are pounded with a lump of wood in a bucket: not a job for the squeamish. Bran is then mixed in with this lumpy paste and oil added until the texture is fairly firm. Dried blood is a somewhat redundant luxury. Some 10 lb (4.5 kg) of mixture is then tied into an open-weave onion sack and hung astern so that it only gives out goodness when a wave slops it. Most of the sack should be above the water line, else the mixture will run out too fast.

Baits are streamed astern—generally two or three mackerel—fishing about 30 yd (30 m) behind the boat, where the shallowest one will be, with the deeper baits further back. Each should be separated by about 10 yd (10 m) of sea to eliminate tangles. The baits are set to fish at different depths, with about one fathom between each one. Traces are suspended by tying thread round the line at the selected depth. This is then tied to a partially-inflated child's balloon. Each angler should fish a different colour. Old washing-up liquid bottles can be used, but balloons are best. They should be inflated no larger than a grapefruit or a taking fish may be spooked at the drag it creates when it pulls the float under.

Baits can be rigged in various ways. Major sharks like a largish bait: one mackerel threaded up onto the hook-shank and up the line, another hooked through the eye sockets and allowed to hang in the hook's bend. Live baits can also be fished in tandem. Fix a couple of small split-rings where the wire is crimped to the hook. Then fix a small clip to each one. A pair of lively mackerel is then clipped through the lower jaw. Because mackerel are shoal fish, they tend to swim in the same direction. This is why the fish in a group of mackerel on a set of feathers do not swim in different directions until about to be hauled into the boat.

When a run comes, the float may bob a few times

A Sussex tope that weighed in at 60 lb (27 kg).

before diving away. Sometimes a porgie will try to eat the balloon, and will look most offended when one bursts in its mouth. When a fish has taken a bait, it sets off on a run. Let it go, with the reel in free spool, and a thumb hovering above it in case of over-run. When it stops, it will be turning the bait before swallowing it. When it moves off again, the bait should be well inside the mouth and a hefty strike should be made. Wind in slack as fast as possible until the fish is felt, then thump the hook home hard. It should be needle-sharp, of course. Wind tight and thump home again. Do this once more for luck. Just as the fish takes off in fury, thumb down on the spool so that the extra pressure ensures that the hook has gone home properly, then let the fish have its head, fighting the rod's spring and the reel's drag until tired enough to be brought to the boat and released.

Tope tactics are different. The same rubby-dubby mixture can be used. However, if the water is deep, it pays to fix the sack close to the sea-bed. Under these circumstances it can pay to use a bag made up from chicken wire to hold the sack, to prevent greedy fish trying to eat the bag, thereby destroying it and your trail. Another method is to lower a 10 lb (4.5 kg) weight on another line. This is housed on a small

Male pack tope go crazy on whispy tackle. Tail small fish aboard, but grip bigger specimens around a pectoral fin.

winch, like those used for loading boats on trailers, but with a large arbor of foam-filled glass fibre. The line is 100 lb (45 kg) test stainless steel fishing line. This fine stuff cuts through the tide. The bag is then weighted with 3 lb (1.35 kg) of lead and allowed to slide on a loop tied round the wire line. Thus it can easily be retrieved and replenished as the day wears on. When the tide turns it is wise to pull the lines up off the sea-bed in case they snag while the boat drifts from one position to another.

Tope feed on the bottom and prefer baits presented on a long trace. I use a whole mackerel as this tends to defeat the rapacity of dogfish. Cut off the bait's tail to prevent it twirling in the tide, then thread the hook up to its head, leaving the bend standing proud from one gill-cover. Tie this into position with elastic thread which is wound round the fish, then round the hook for a couple of turns, then round the fish and so on until it is locked into position. Before dropping the bait overboard it pays to slice its flank so as to release that all-important scent of blood. With the sinker fixed to the line via a boom, the weight is kept on board while the bait is streamed astern. Between the boom and the trace slides a length of PVC flex cover. When the desired trace length is reached, a matchstick is jammed into this flex cover, thereby stopping the weight. This system is superior to the match-stick and clove-hitch, which often weakens the line so much that it snaps on the strike.

Tope will also take live mackerel fixed near the sea-

bed. Thread the hook very carefully between a bait's eyeball and its socket and through a hole in the skull which connects both eyes, then back out of the other socket. This trick keeps mackerel alive for hours. Sometimes tope will take them in preference to dead baits.

Trolling is a neglected technique in British seas. It works sometimes with porbeagles. The trick is to tease them into taking a bait by trailing a string of a dozen mackerel on a separate line astern of the boat. The backbone of these teasers and of the bait is removed so that the fish swim in what looks like a lifelike manner. Any curious sharks will nip free offerings off the daisy-chain. When it becomes confident of what it is doing—especially as no hook is inside these teasers—a baited trace is dropped astern to it and the teasers pulled aboard. Slow trolling speeds are more effective than the 10–20 knots used by tropical big-game trollers.

Few people would claim that shark meat is delicious—indeed, that of the Greenland shark, when fresh, is poisonous. So there can be no justification in killing them. Let them go with a minimum of fuss at the boatside, so that stocks are not depleted. Surely an angler's ego is no valid justification for the slaughter of one of these magnificent, ancient beasts.

AUTUMN: CONGER

Sea serpents do not come in any more frightening shapes than the conger eel. It has inspired some horrific tales over the years. It looks as though it could slither around, biting lumps out of boats and crushing sturdy gaff handles between its powerful jaws. It also looks as though it is capable of putting the evil eye on its unfortunate captor. However, as most conger fishermen start out by fearing the fish before they even catch it, such an attitude is unlikely to be changed when the two meet face to face. In fact, the species is shy and retiring by nature. It shuns bright light and spends its time hiding away in the densest cover it can find: wrecks, rugged reefs and similar places where it can lead a quiet life. Anglers refer to such habitat as a lair, with all the wicked intent such a den implies. It is because of the way this fish shuns publicity that a great deal of mystery and mythology surrounds it. Neither do scientists have much luck in unravelling its life story.

It is suspected that congers grow quite fast. Captive eels have grown to about 90 lb (40 kg) within an estimated five years from birth. However, it has proved very hard to follow the life of an eel from egg to death because of the unusual nature of its lifestyle. Mature eels migrate over the Continental shelf to spawn somewhere between Gibraltar and the Sargasso

Sea, in mid-water, at depths of around 2000 fathoms—over 2¼ miles (3.6 km) down. The larvae drift back to our shores and metamorphose into tiny congers. They then feed on anything from crabs to small fish, to large fish, until nature tells them to restart the cycle. For congers, sex is a once-and-forever experience. They migrate before they reach sexual maturity for this reason. Developing roes suck so much substance from their bodies that their teeth fall out, the alimentary tract and other organs degenerate and the skeleton decalcifies—not the best state in which to start a long journey. Consequently, mature eels, ripe for spawning, have never been caught. The above observations have been made on specimens that lived out their lives in aquaria.

Male congers grow to around 3 ft (90 cm) in length, so obviously anglers are more interested in the giant mommas which grow to around 150 lb (68 kg)—possibly more with sterile specimens.

Rough ground is the place to find these eels. However, when autumn approaches and the fish feed up for winter, many are caught over open ground while tagging behind shoals of migrating baitfish. Congers close to land do not migrate out to deep water with the onset of severe weather, but stay where they are and become torpid. In very severe weather, fish dwelling in shallow water may be chilled to death and washed ashore. Sometimes, after a cold spell, the fish are to be found drifting in a comatose state close to the surface, where commercial fishermen gaff them aboard. In the deep, where the water temperature changes less severely, congers remain active throughout the year, though they feed less in winter.

Autumn, then, offers some of the best opportunities to the boat angler. However, congers can be caught throughout the warm months of the year, though the fall is regarded as the time for the best catches.

A popular misconception is that very stout tackle is required for bringing these fish to the boat. And so it is if you startle them into fighting while they are still within striking distance of their lairs. The fact is that this eel is just a little dim. If you use a stealthy approach, the fish will not realize that it is in danger until too late.

The trick is to seduce the fish from its stronghold, after you get a bite, by gently winding in line—winding the fish onto the hook. Because congers are reluctant to let go of a bait, the fish will allow itself to be led for many yards until the penny drops. I have caught them on extremely light tackle from the shore (of only 20 lb [9 kg], to be sure), but in each case the fish has allowed itself to be reeled in without any protest until the last moment.

Even 12 lb (5.50 kg) class outfits can be used for

Conger eel.

small fish up to about 20 lb (9 kg). When after moderate fish, 20–30 lb (9–14 kg) outfits can be employed. When real heavyweights are expected from deep-water wrecks, 50 lb (23 kg) class rods, reels and lines should be used because the angler requires a stiff rod to lever the fish up in the water. Under these conditions, the tide helps the angler. By carefully winding the fish onto the hook, and not spooking it through a hefty strike, the fish can be drawn well away from the wreck. By the time it realizes its mistake, it will be in open water above the wreck. Congers are certainly not built for speed. The fish cannot dive into the tide and regain the security of the structure,

because it is hanging from the hook with its entire flank exposed to the current. This pushes it well away from the structure, even lifting it in the water. These factors cause problems at the boat. The fish fights by backing away, with a few arm-wrenching jolts, from rod pressure. When it is lying exhausted at the surface, the pressure of both tide and large eel can make it very difficult to draw the fish towards the boat. This is when lines part, hook-holds give way, and hooks snap under the strain.

Most conger anglers prefer to use a reel with a low gearing ratio. This is more efficient at hauling, even though standard pumping techniques should be used most of the time. However, the angler should keep the fish's head turned towards the boat, and pumping can allow it to turn back to the bottom if there is not much current running. So a reel that can double as a winch is often an advantage.

Carefully-constructed terminal rigs are essential for congers because of the strain imposed during the closing stages of the fight. Knots must be very strong and totally reliable. The end-rig need not be complicated; just a standard leger tackle is adequate. Many anglers now use heavy-gauge commercial nylon for traces instead of wire. Nylon is more supple, not liable to damage due to kinking, and is easier to work with. It also provides a more secure grip when a large fish needs to be dragged from one part of a boat to another. Congers do not have particularly fierce teeth, although their jaws are very powerful, so the heavy-gauge nylon is adequate to cope with the abrasion.

Most anglers fit a Clements boom onto the main line and tie a strong clip to the end. The sinker is tied on with weak line in case it catches in the snaggy ground that congers call home. The trace is made up with a strong swivel at one end and a size 6/0 to 10/0 hook at the other. This species has a large mouth, so baits should be selected that appeal through size as well as flavour. Big baits should be mounted on big hooks.

If you have not yet used commercial nylon traces, you may not know that the method of fixing them to swivel and hook is with crimps, as used with wire. However, do not try to squash the crimps flat as this will severely weaken the trace. The best system is to flatten the crimp partially, then squeeze it tight at the edges only. This will prevent the nylon from slipping. Even so, until you become confident in your workmanship, test each trace thoroughly.

Hooks must be tough—Mustad Seamasters are about the best available in the UK, although if you visit a tackle emporium in the United States of America you will come across a wide range of hooks that are designed for tuna, marlin and other tough-spirited gamefish, and which are often superior in design for congers. Whatever make you choose, test one or two from the batch to destruction. Tie one to a tree's branch; tie a loop of thin rope round a heavy weight and hang this from the hook. Jiggle it up and down a few times to see how much pressure it takes before it shows signs of strain, and whether it snaps without warning or will bend appreciably before snapping. Temper varies in hooks between batches. The best ones will cope with untold abuse before giving in. Do not bother with swivelled conger hooks. They are inferior in design to others. The swivel is not efficient, so is an unnecessary hinderance to the careful mounting of a bait.

Use a small triangular file for honing the inside of the point and barb to a cutting edge, and the point to the sharpness of a needle. If the barb is too large and rank for smooth penetration, file it down somewhat. This applies to all sea fishing hooks. Because congers should be wound onto the hook, it is essential that this action should lead to the hook nicking into tissue inside the fish's mouth so that it cannot eject the hook when it realizes its error. Then, when it lunges and you pull back, the hook slides home.

No matter how eager you are to see the fish, stay your hand a while and let the fish thump about down there and tire itself out. Ideally it should be exhausted by the time it hits the surface. There are two reasons for this. First, a lively fish will start spinning with amazing speed when it surfaces. This may be unnerving, but does little damage to tackle. With several yards of line out, the eel would have to spin a great deal before it created sufficient stress on the tackle to weaken it. Even so, it is a sign of a lively fish. Secondly, the gaffman will not thank you if he has to bring aboard a fish that is still full of fight, and other anglers aboard will not be very happy to share the boat with an angry, resentful eel. Flasks and tackle will go flying as the fish thrashes about.

A tired eel is a different matter. The gaffman can carry it on the gaff to the fish hold and dump it there to expire in its own time. Very few boatmen go through the process of clubbing an eel to death. However, the small-boat angler who has less space to work in and limited stowage facilities will prefer to kill his eels. This is done with a billy-club or truncheon. Hit the fish hard across the back, close to the vent. The lymph heart is sited there and a blow on the spot will stun it. Then hit it just behind the eyes, very hard, a couple of times and the fish will swiftly expire.

When congering from my dinghy, I then dump the fish back overboard, but tie the trace to a cleat at the stern, making sure that the fish's head is out of the water so that it cannot revive. Obviously it is unwise to start poking about inside a conger's mouth, no matter how dead it may appear. Unclip the trace and fix on a fresh one. The others can be retrieved at leisure ashore.

Another advantage of the nylon trace, which must appeal to conservationists, is that hooked congers can be released at boatside with one slice of a sharp knife. Most congers have little trouble getting rid of hooks, and scientists have been amazed at the way that deeply-hooked fish have managed to pass hooks through their intestines.

It was once feared that conger stocks could be fished out. However, while it is likely that over-zealous hauling on a productive wreck will severely reduce stocks to the level that bites become rare, a rest of a few months, such as over winter, will see the wreck restock itself. There are so many wrecks and reefs around our coast that it would be impossible to cause lasting damage to the conger population. It is likely that this species is as cyclic as any other, and that years of plenty are followed by lean times. However, the large ladies lay about eight million eggs before they die.

While static baits account for large numbers of congers, it should not be forgotten that this species is an active hunter, using its sinuous, slimy body to slither within striking range of small fish. There are quite a number of people who have caught congers on artificial lures. While wrecking for cod and ling, especially with baited pirks, several congers are hooked each summer. I was out on a wrecking trip once when a colleague hooked into a monster fish, only to lose it when it regained the structure. This happened because he thought it was a cod, and thumped the hook home. It is almost impossible to use standard methods of seducing these eels from wrecks when one is fishing pirks.

The same friend hooked into another on the next drift through. It, too, snagged up. We decided, because the snag kept giving a little, that one of his cod feathers had caught into a cable or something similar down there. So he slackened off for the fish to free itself, which it did. This was after spending some ten minutes trying to haul it clear—something that is worth remembering if it happens to you. Anyway, when the fish was brought to the boat it was found to have missed the pirk and to have taken one of the feathers. The skipper was unlucky enough to get another feather embedded into his thumb soon after gaffing the 40 lb (18 kg) fish aboard. Fortunately the conger was pretty tired by then, otherwise the incident would have been even more painful.

Other anglers fish specifically for congers using baited attractor spoons. However, I am forced to wonder whether such tactics are strictly necessary. Do they produce more fish than standard bottom-fishing with bait? I believe not. Congers are fitted with the most amazingly sensitive nostrils. They can pick up minute dilutions of plasma in the water and home in on them.

Conger baits should always, therefore, be very fresh. They will occasionally take a piece of rotten bait, but they prefer fresh, bleeding baits most of the time. However, kipper is a favourite along some parts of the coast and pieces of mackerel and herring that have been allowed to mature for a day in a warm place have been known to do well. They glow a luminous green colour, caused by decomposition, which must assist the fish in finding its way to the bait.

Squid, cuttlefish, herring, mackerel and similar fare are preferred by most congers. Pouting, which are generally large and abundant over wrecks, make very good baits. Many anglers prefer pouting to mackerel. Such large baits should be mounted on the hook so that they ooze body fluids. My favourite method when fishing for large conger is to take off a rough fillet from one side of a pouting, discard this and mount the rest of the fish. However, no matter what bait is used, there comes a time when most of its scent is washed out. If you have not had a bite within, say, twenty minutes, reel in and drop down again.

A good boatman is essential for congering. This is because eels will be reluctant to swim too far from the structure to take a bait. Wrecks and reefs should be precisely located—a good boatman will tell you how far astern the fishing area is located. The anglers then clip on sinkers that will fall directly into this zone or which can be trotted back there with the tide.

Never be in a hurry to react to a conger bite. They take their time and will often mouth and reject a bait repeatedly before moving off with it. Then is the time to react. If the fish does not have the bait inside its mouth when you start reeling it towards the boat it is quite likely to follow, even up to the boatside (in shallow water) before letting go of it.

Braided or wire line is useful for congering because it is more sensitive. If you feel your sinker being dragged over the sea-bed you can then be sure the fish has taken the bait properly.

Wire line has tremendous advantages when used in deep water and strong tides, but it can be difficult to use unless certain precautions are taken. Because it has inherent weight, it does not require much lead to take the bait down to the fish. And because it does not stretch at all, the smallest bites can be felt with ease—even the nibbles of tiddlers. However, it is springy and will bound into a mass of loose coils if treated wrong. Care must be taken to spool it back neatly onto the reel. And it should be paid out cautiously to prevent an over-run and loose coils, which can kink and weaken it. A nylon leader is essential so that it can be broken free in case of snagging.

Because it is so fine for its strength, 100 yd (100 m) can be wound onto an Ambassadeur 7000 reel over a bed of nylon and will not take up much space. This reel's level-wind system ensures that the line is re-wound carefully, even when a fish is distracting your attention. One trick for maintaining pressure on the spool, thus preventing loose coils from springing up, is to obtain a typewriter cleaning brush, grind down the central bristles on a wheel so that they hug the spool efficiently, and screw this between the reel's shoe and the spool. These brushes have a wooden back, and readily accept small screws.

Wire line has no stretch, so the nylon leader provides elasticity which prevents excessive strain from tearing the hooks out of the fish. Its elasticity also allows you to reel in until the swivel on the end of the trace jambs in the rod's tip-ring. With several turns of nylon on the spool and the tension taken up on the leader, there is no way that loose coils can pop up when the rod is lain down; and the brush takes care of tension while a bait is down there.

The best way to join wire to nylon is to form a loop in the nylon—a Bimini loop is strongest—and then take two turns of the wire round this and crimp the loose end to the main part of the line. These turns must be very small and tight to the nylon, or they will spring into a figure-of-eight shape. The crimp should be the smallest possible. The loose end should be cut off flush with the end of the crimp so that no tiny stubs of wire can cut fingers. Some anglers prefer to twist both the loose end and the standing part together into a series of open turns before tightening up the crimp.

Congers are not too hard to hook and land, but anglers who go afloat in their own boats are likely to have trouble in locating suitable fishing areas. The best locations are rugged reefs and wrecks. Navigational skills help here in taking bearings from land and sea marks so that the right ground can be fished with pinpoint accuracy. While it is possible to spend a small fortune on fish location systems, much can be learnt from careful use of a simple echo-sounder.

Wrecks, for example, can be located by shore marks if they are not too far out. Once in the area, if the sea is calm, a boil will be noticed some way down-tide from the structure. This comes about because the current is forced towards the surface by the obstruction. The boatman then motors up-tide from the boil until the wreck shows on his echo-sounder. He then continues for 100 yd (100 m) or so and drops a dan-buoy. Once this has settled, he runs round the buoy until he has picked up the wreck—or rocks—on his echo-sounder, and then works out how the structure is lying in relation to the tide and to the buoy. With experience it is fairly simple to work out how far up-tide the anchor should be dropped so that, when the boat has settled, the baits can be presented correctly on the edge of the structure. Many anglers leave the buoy out there overnight if the fishing is good and the weather promises to remain fair, cutting out the hassle of locating it again next day. Even so, it is sensible to check that the buoy has not shifted during the night and that the tide direction is the same as it was the previous day.

Congers are said to bite best when the weather is still and thundery. I am not so sure of this. They do not like cold weather when close to shore, and they dislike very strong light. Catches in shallow water are generally best at night. However, there is always the possi-

Conger and dogfish dumped after a fishing match.

bility that a structure will be relatively under-populated during the hours of darkness because its residents will be out hunting. In deepish water—say twenty fathoms—the eels do not seem too bothered because so little light penetrates to those depths anyway in British waters. One thing they do not like, however, is strong currents. Best catches tend to come on neap tides, though this may happen because the fishing is easier, too. As with all other fishing matters, only experience on site can provide finite answers to these and related problems.

WINTER: COD

Winter boat fishing is not for the faint-hearted. The weather is often so poor for days at a time that skippers put to sea even when there is a force 5 wind blowing: calm by comparison with what has gone before. With a chill wind, icy spray and no sun, the air out there feels as if it has come straight from Siberia. By contrast, there are days of weak sunshine and calm, sparkling seas, and it is possible to feel too warm inside one's swaddles. The wise angler dresses very warmly for winter boat fishing, wearing all the modern thermal undies that are available, and stays cheerful while those about him turn blue and rigid. For all this, winter codding has a gutsy appeal that few anglers can resist, especially when the weather is kind. And, for good measure, it is a sport that can be had from small boats, close to land. Very often the best codding lies within a mile of the shoreline and there is nothing to be gained from driving off to the horizon.

Small-boat fishing is a delightful way of spending a day—summer or winter. One has complete freedom to fish wherever one wants and can pack up whenever one loses interest. Most boats are comfortable with just two, maybe three people aboard. Small-boat codding has the advantage that in many areas there is little to be gained by zooming for miles out to sea or along the coast, so less fuel is burnt than is the case when being more ambitious in summer.

Boat-handling demands certain skills which can only be learnt through practice. The newcomer is advised to go with an experienced handler before he attempts to go out on his own. An American boating writer describes acquiring the skills of handling as a 'seat of the pants experience.' This means that you can only learn how to accomplish certain manoeuvres by getting afloat and learning it all first hand. This author did just that, sometimes finding himself in tricky situations, with sheer terror teaching the finer points of running and beaching in rough weather.

Winter dinghy fishing requires preparation and skill. The sea is very cold, so launching must be undertaken with precision as nothing is more unpleasant than sitting out there with waders full of water. Watch any experienced crew, and you will appreciate that every last detail of preparation is taken care of before they put to sea. Oars are stowed in rowlocks, ready for action. The engine is connected to the fuel and ready to start. When a swell is running, it is essential to look at the waves about 100 yd (100 m) out and to watch for a calm spell. Then is the time to launch. Float the boat, have the oarsman in position, then push off. If the swell is tricky, take one oar yourself and synchronize your movements.

Some launchings are hilariously incompetent. Flailing oars drive the boat through half a circle and it then risks being broached by a big wave. However, a few full-chested pulls of the oars should carry any boat out behind the surf line, where the engine can be started at leisure. However, if the breeze is coming into the beach, or even if it is coming along it, one man should stay at the oars so that the boat is not drifted into trouble.

Beaching can be hazardous. Planing hulls are generally easy to beach. Just drive in with the throttle wide, cut and tilt the engine at the last second and the boat should fly ashore under its own momentum. This beats heaving the thing out of the water. Displacement hulls cannot do this, so the boatman runs in on a big wave and the craft is then hauled from the water. Many fishing clubs who use these craft have regular beaching and launching sites so that members can assist each other. I have watched boats being plucked from rough seas after the craft got into difficulties at the edge. Five strong men can wade in and haul the boat well out of reach of the breakers. However, this is hard to do if the thing is full of water. This problem can be solved by replacing the tiny drainage bung with two 2 in (5 cm) bath plugs that fit into specially-made holes, one on each side of the stern. The water pours back out of these after a wave has slopped aboard. A fairly deep, tapering hole ensures that the plugs can be jammed hard home. A loose plug can be knocked out by a breaking wave. It is wise to tie the things to a handy staple or eye with heavy fishing line—and to carry spares. My own boat is a planing hull, but even these can be foxed by heavy surf and arrive at the beach with insufficient momentum for that final slide to safety. Once, in my very green days, we ran out of fuel just 200 yd (200 m) from our home beach. We had to row ashore. As soon as the boat bumped the shingle, it stopped. A following wave filled the craft, soaking us, and our catch of big bass started floating over the transom and back out to sea. Hence the bath plugs. Hence, too, the value of seat-of-the-pants experience, and a spare can of fuel.

Winter cod fishing requires good bait. With the fish close to shore, there is little point in using large pirks and similar hardware, because the sea is generally so murky that the fish cannot see them. Neither are they shoaled up into tight-packed groups as often as they are over summer wrecks. The fish are usually more scattered, the shoals extending over several hundred yards as they move along the coast hunting for crabs, small fish and similar fare.

As with all fishing, it pays to listen out for reports of catches by other anglers. This is more valuable than scanning the pages of angling publications, and checking out catch reports which may be three weeks out of date. Cultivate a grapevine so that you are among the very first to hear of any decent catches. Winter cod are generally migrating fish. They move along the coast and large shoals may linger in one spot for only a few days. In very good years the inshore waters seem to be overrun with cod and it then makes little difference where you fish; with, of course, the obvious proviso that there are certain recognized marks where the fish

The joys of beach-landing (and launching)!

linger, or group together. As wreckers demonstrate, the more fish there are in one area, the more you catch.

A 12 or 20 lb (5.50 or 9 kg) class outfit is quite adequate for general boat codding, whether you go in your own dinghy or in a charter boat. The fine lines used with such rigs cut through the water well and require less lead to get a bait down to the fish. Anglers who fish 30 lb (14 kg) line for cod may require 1–1½ lb (450–700 g) of lead to get down there. This sort of tackle is insensitive and very often the angler has such difficulty hauling his sinker back into the boat that he is unaware that a 5 lb (2.25 kg) fish is on the end. In very shallow water some anglers go down to 6 lb (2.70 kg) outfits and experience immense fun with run-of-the-mill specimens.

Coarse fishermen are often better at sea fishing than regular sea anglers. This is because they have to choose their lines with care. The fish can see the line, but a certain strength is required to bring it to net, so they strike a very fine balance between these two points. Thus they are very skilled at feeling how much pressure they can put onto a hooked fish without popping the line. Sea anglers generally appear to be less sensitive to these finer points of tackle handling and, as a result, lose out on good, clean sporting fun. This comes to mind after chatting with a friend who is a very good coarse angler. He had just come back from a trip to Torquay where he had met someone in a pub and had been invited out for a day's fishing. On his

carp rod and line he took conger to 20 lb (9 kg), thornbacks to 17 lb (7.50 kg) and a host of lesser species.

It is becoming increasingly obvious that sea fish can be wary of baits that act in an unnatural manner. When there are vast numbers of fish about and they are in competition with each other, their instinct is to grab a bait before one of their shoal-mates gets to it. However, such days are less frequent than they used to be. No healthy sea fish ever died of starvation; there is too much food for them in the sea. If something about the way a bait has been presented arouses their suspicion, they are quite likely to swim away from it.

If you can use very light and sensitive tackle, then do so. You will have more fun and will probably catch more fish. This has been proved to me with species like plaice and bass. Also, because cod are dour fighters when hooked from a boat, the light tackle enables them to show their mettle.

When fishing from a small boat, which causes less disturbance in the sea than a large charter boat, many anglers fish right behind the craft, trotting their bait down the tide, away from the hull. The further away the bait is from the boat, the more direct is contact between bait and rod. If the bait is right underneath, a fish must give a hefty pull for the rod to do much more than nod a few times. Moreover, the further the bait is downtide, the more easy it is to set the hook. And the line is not in a bow, but almost straight.

The way to achieve this is simple. Fix on a lead that is light enough to be trotted down the tide. When you lift the rod-tip after dropping down a bait, the sinker

A 22 lb (10 kg) October cod, his first of the winter season: ample reason to look smug.

will be lifted up from the bottom. With the reel in free-spool, a few yards of line can be paid out until the sinker is felt to hit bottom again. Wind in any slack, or until you feel the weight, then lift the rod up high above your head and repeat the process. A time will come when it is impossible to pay out any more line. This is because there is no bow in the line and contact to the bait is virtually direct.

This trick has other advantages, too. It allows the angler to walk his bait up and down the sand bars until he locates the feeding area of fish. It also allows him to trot his tackle back to the edge of a reef, or into a wreck or whatever. With braided line, the operation is very sensitive. You can feel the bottom through this line and, with experience, can tell whether your sinker is walking over sand, weeds, rock or even the structure of a wreck.

If you are feeling energetic you can also try boat-casting from a small boat, with maybe a couple of rods per angler fishing out to each side. This idea is often vital to success when a charter boat is used because the hull creates off-putting disturbance in the water and, some skippers believe, the tide drumming on the anchor warp is amplified by the hull, which acts like a sounding box. This disturbance spooks fish; they steer clear of it. However, these fish can be contacted by belting baits out to each side of the boat. And your spread of baits is covering an area that is very much wider than is the case when trotting baits astern. The result is increased catches.

If fish are scarce, many anglers fish one boat-caster each and one rod down-tide from a small boat. If there are not many anglers on a big boat, two boat-casters can be managed with ease. However, much depends here on the attitude of the skipper.

Boat-casting is essentially beach-casting in a strong tide, but from a less stable platform and with less emphasis on distance. A 5 or 6 oz (150 or 180 g) wired torpedo sinker is used: lighter if you can get away with it. In moderate currents the break-out versions are best, while fierce tides can be counteracted with grapnel leads, the wires coming out of the nose and extending for a couple of inches before being turned back like anchor flukes. Unfortunately these often grip the sea-bed so tenaciously that a fierce bite is required to dislodge them. For example, I was once fishing with my twelve-year-old nephew and he was boat-casting for small fish while I was trotting a bait away down tide for tope. He reeled in half a pouting that must have originally weighed 1½ lb (700 g). It had been chopped by a tope, but no indication of this event had been visible at his rod-top.

The ideal rod for this technique is shorter than a beach-caster: around 10 ft (3.05 m). It should be of fast-taper construction, but with a very fine tip, like many ultra-modern beach-casters. Too long a rod is nothing but a nuisance in a boat, and makes landing fish less than simple. A standard beach reel can be used, together with 10–15 lb (4.50–6.75 kg) line, or less if you feel you can handle it.

The terminal outfit, which is generally similar to that used from the beach, is then belted away from the boat and up-tide, so that the sinker can grip into the bottom. However, as with beach-fishing, a large loop of line is let out so that the axis of the lead is the same as that of the boat. The tide, acting on this loop, holds the sinker in position. Several anglers can cast to different positions around the boat, the prow being the favoured spot if no seas are running.

A slender tip will bow over to the tide's pull and, when a fish dislodges the sinker, will spring straight as the weight trundles down-tide. Wind in until the fish is felt, then sink the hook.

With experience, you will find that you can boat-cast in up to 100 ft (30 m) of water. Much depends on the tide's strength. Obviously, if a strong push of water is coming through, you will have to cast a long way up-tide so that the weight grips bottom before it is swept past the boat.

This technique can be dangerous in inexperienced hands. It is essential that the tackle is dangled outside the boat before casting it high overhead so that it does not hit anybody or catch on tackle bags, spare sweaters and parts of the boat. It is wise to warn everybody when you are casting so that they can watch out for themselves. When casting well up past the boat's prow, it is impossible to dangle the tackle overboard unless you move right to the boat's stern. Many anglers learn to cast while facing away from the direction they will be casting, and hurl the tackle over their shoulder so that they can keep an eye on it while it is a danger to other anglers. It does not take very much learning.

Boat-casting is also effective when wind is blowing against the tide and the boat is swinging to and fro on its anchor. The loop of line has sufficient play in it to cope with this movement and the tackle is not dragged about over the sea bed.

No matter what tackle or tactics are employed, one aspect is constant: good bait. Although groundbaiting with crushed shellfish and similar feed would probably be effective if employed in the manner advocated for tope, a good cod bait is usually sufficient to bring fish in from afar. This means that it must be a large, juicy lump of organic material. Most anglers are aware how easy it is to fit a fist into the mouth of even a 10 lb (4.5 kg) cod. There is no reason why angler's baits should not be equally large.

Cocktails make the best cod baits. Bunches of lugworm, mussels, razorfish, slipper limpets, soft crab, fresh fish and squid all account for good specimens. It pays to create such baits at home, if you can, rather than fiddle about in a choppy sea and freeze your fingers in the process. Ideally a successful trip will start with a lugworm-digging session. These worms are the basis of all successful cod cocktails and you will need plenty. As supplies in winter are unreliable and costly, the wise angler buys himself a fork or lugging spade and learns how to do it himself. The skill will pay dividends.

The most reliable type of cocktail for any conditions should include half a dozen large black lug and half a dozen large razorfish. Other items can be added to taste. These are laid out alongside each other, rolled into a bundle, then tied together with either wool or elastic thread. The result is then lashed to a 6/0 or 8/0 hook, with the complete bend protruding from one side.

This may sound a waste of good bait. However, experience shows that the resultant strong scent trail brings in fish very quickly. Once hooked, the cod has only to shake its head a few times, which very few ever fail to do, and the sausage is pushed up the line and out of danger. On unhooking the fish, the bait is then slid back onto the hook, given a good squeeze to release more juices, and sent back down to the fish.

If you still think that this is excessive, just reflect on the story that lies behind those huge 30–40 lb (14–18 kg) cod that are caught each winter from The Needles area off the Isle of Wight. Large squids are used, around 1 ft (30.5 cm) long. These are mounted on what freshwater men call a Pennell tackle—two hooks tied to a length of line with about 6 in (15 cm) between each. The fish are attracted by this big, white, scented bait flickering and rolling in the tide.

You may care to try a trick that has brought plenty of good fish of many species into boats, including tope, turbot and cod. Obtain a small white bucket and cut a large willow-leaf shape from one side, or several to replace any that are lost. Fix one of these shapes on a swivel about 1 ft (30.5 cm) or so ahead of the bait. Giant baited spoons like this are very effective at times—especially with halibut.

Cod are among the most efficient predators in the sea. No matter where the food is most abundant, they are there in the midst of it. With huge eyes, a super-sensitive vibration detection system, and taste buds in their mouth, on their barbel and fin rays, little escapes their attention.

This is why live baits are so effective at attracting them. The same trick can be used from boats as is employed from the beach. Make up a two-hook rig.

Both hooks can be baited: the larger with a sausage of bait lashed aboard, the smaller with a single large worm. Pouting and whiting will be attracted by the seductive scent of the bait, if a cod does not get there first, and will take the straggly length of worm. Then you will have the bait to beat them all, vibrations from a panicking, hooked fish alongside a heavily-scented attractor.

Baits like those described above are not always necessary, however. There are days when so many cod are about that only a couple of lugworm on a size 4/0 hook will catch them. But the old adage of big baits for big fish will always hold true. A sure way of sorting hefty specimens from average fish is to load the hooks generously.

Another technique scores well with cod, and a variety of other species, throughout the year. This involves fitting a set of standard cod feathers to the end of the main line, sometimes with a pirk instead of a lead weight. The feathers are baited with fish strip, lugworm, squid and so on.

This type of tackle is ideal for fishing mixed ground: patches of reef, rubble and sand. The gear is gently jigged close to the sea-bed and accounts for large numbers of fish, though mainly smallish ones. It is widely used in those parts of the country where small fish are abundant and can be caught three or four at a time.

While drifting over a favoured mark, it soon becomes apparent, through the bursts of activity, that the cod prefer specific patches. If a really hot area is found, this should be noted and returned to. However, one of the problems with drifting is that it is not always easy to return to precisely the same mark each time unless there are excellent shore marks to use as bearings and obvious features on the sea bed that show up on the echo-sounder. Under conditions of fast tides, with the boat drifting for several hundred yards while a stringful of fish is brought to the surface, accuracy can be difficult to achieve when running back to the hot-spot.

If you are confident that the fish will not move from the area, drop a buoy overboard the moment you hit fish. This need be no more than a heavy sinker tied to a reel of old line that is fixed inside a frame. A length of line from the frame goes to a 1 gal (3.75 l) plastic bottle. On the next drift drop another buoy up-tide from the original marker, then either retrieve or cut loose the first one. This is because that marker will be sitting just downtide from where the fish are. While drifting from the main (the second) buoy down to the fish, there is every chance that lines of hooked fish will become tangled round the original marker. Thus fish and tackle will be lost, or at least badly tangled.

This reminds me of a time when I fished with friends

A fair brace of cod caught by this angleress with up-tide boat-casting techniques.

for a large shoal of cod over a deep-water reef with a very fast tide running over it. We knew the fish were down there, but could not locate them for about half an hour. Then an eruption of sprats at the surface, and attendant activity by herring gulls, showed us where they were feeding. Quickly we motored over and began a drift through the area. Fish hit our rigs so fast that all three of us ended up with full houses of cod. So I threw over a buoy. The same happened next drift after we had aligned ourselves with the buoy. Trouble was that we lost two sets of tackle to the buoy line. We could not move it because that would defeat our powers of fish location. So we had to drift to one side of the shoal instead. We caught plenty, but as we did not have a second buoy, we missed out on making a major haul. On another occasion we found that our buoy was not correctly placed, but it was sufficient to show where we should be drifting: some 50 yd (50 m) to the north of it. So not only does such a marker show where a shoal is sited, but it also enables you to work round it, probing to see how large the shoal is and how much ground it is covering.

One point here on working feathers may be of assistance. Very often anglers catch most cod when they get tired. I, and others, have observed this on charter boats. In moderately deep water, up to about twenty fathoms, anglers who jig pirks and feathers with an extravagance of movement are likely to catch few fish. While such movement may be vital to impart even a little motion to pirks fished at sixty fathoms, the motion is excessive for twenty fathoms. However, as these anglers become dispirited and put less effort into their pirking, so the fish become interested. I have had my best catches in twenty fathoms and under while jigging my pirks and feathers very gently, often moving the rod tip no more than 2–3 ft (60–90 cm). This is also much more sensitive, enabling you to bounce bottom, feeling what is going on down there and the preliminary taps of a shy taker.

Another mistake many people make is to haul their pirk up in the water, then drop the rod-tip, allowing the line to go slack. This is the best way of getting snagged into the sea-bed. Always lower the rod fairly slowly, feeling the tackle back down so that if a pinnacle of reef is down there, you can reel up line and clear it.

This careful feeling of the pirk—or sinker—is essential when drifting over sand-banks and ledges. The fish will be close to the bottom. If you know that the sea-bed drops away over the direction of your drift, keep the reel in free spool, with a thumb on the spool, and pay out line every so often so that the tackle taps bottom from time to time, ensuring that you are fishing in the fish's feeding zone. If a reef shallows up to a ledge and drop-off, a very popular bottom configuration for many species, reel in line every time you tap bottom to prevent it getting snagged.

Surface water drifts faster than that close to the sea-bed, especially if there is a breeze. This may make you drift faster than the current. If so, make yourself a large drogue (sea anchor) and drop it over the bow so that the boat drifts stern-first, with the prow facing into the waves. This will defeat wind drift, especially when the breeze is maddeningly across the tide and it becomes almost impossible to line up on a hot spot with any degree of accuracy. It is also unwise to use too many feathers or lures down there, or line that is too thick. The best way to work lures is to have them fishing straight under the boat. If they stream behind the boat, the action may be more true to life, but the hooks will be perfectly positioned for snagging into the sea-bed. Moreover, by fishing away from the boat, with a mass of lures, baits, feathers and thick line, the whole situation becomes so confused that it is almost impossible to feel what is going on down there until you either snag up or a fish takes.

Winter cod may not always be around when you get afloat, so it sometimes makes sense to take out a set of mackerel feathers with you and bait them for whiting. Do not jamb chunks of fish flesh onto the hooks, but use carefully-cut strips of mackerel or squid that can be mounted to the hooks so that the bait assumes the stream-lined contours of the feathers. You will, in fact, be doing what big-game hunters do in tropical seas: fixing a fluttering skirt ahead of a dead-bait. You can do the same when pirking, too, by fitting a multi-tentacled plastic squid at the head of the pirk.

Winter cod, however, tend to be more lethargic than they are in summer. Likewise the anglers who fish for them. A big bait that has been carefully placed where it will attract most fish, will allow you to doze in the cabin until a keener lad, still braving the weather out there, shouts that your rod is trying to scramble out of the boat.

Success often depends on the amount of thought, rather than energy, that you put into your fishing.

Identification of fish

BROWN TROUT

RAINBOW TROUT

GRAYLING

CHUB

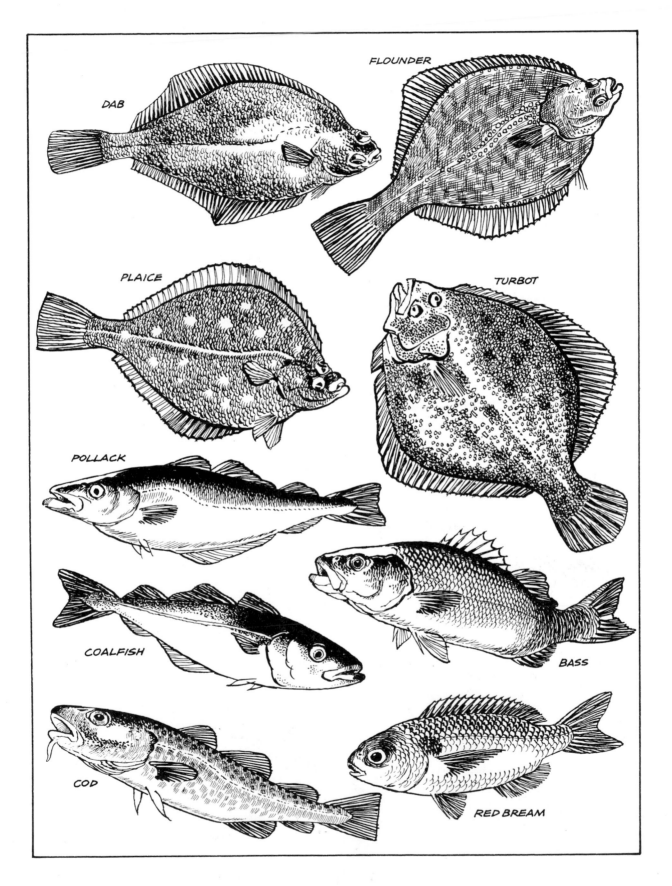

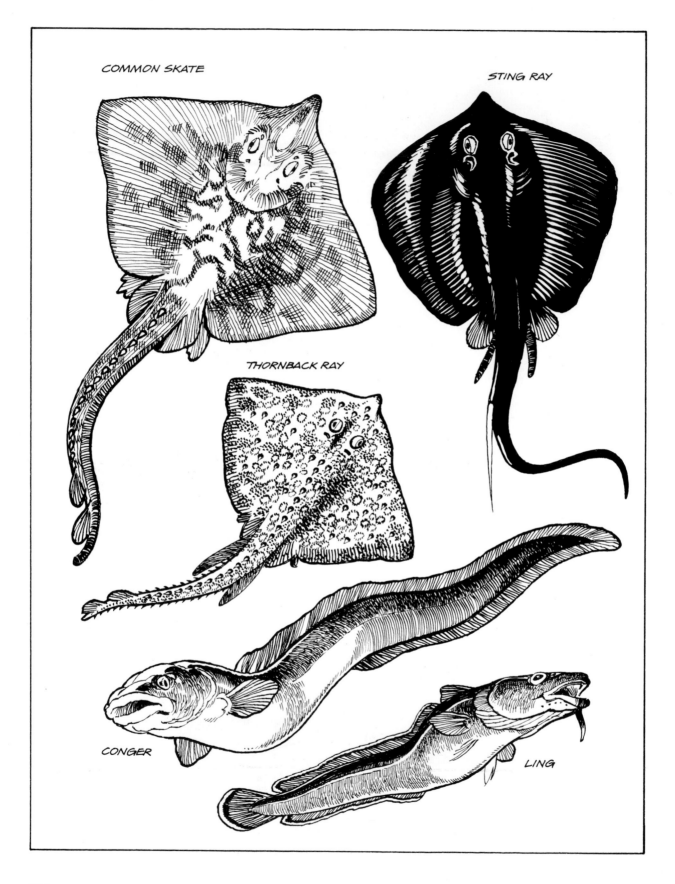

COMMON SKATE

STING RAY

THORNBACK RAY

CONGER

LING

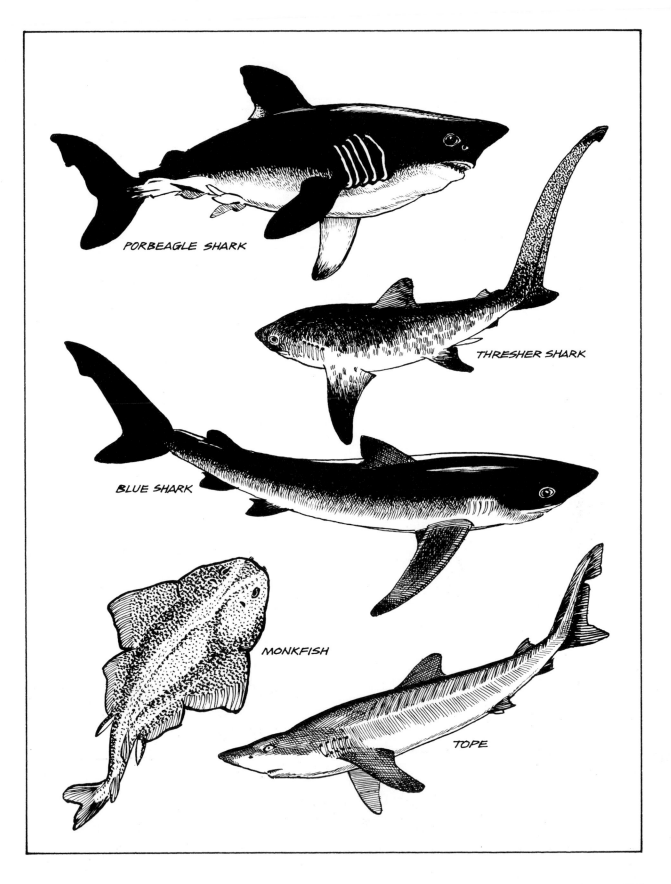

PORBEAGLE SHARK

THRESHER SHARK

BLUE SHARK

MONKFISH

TOPE

Useful knots

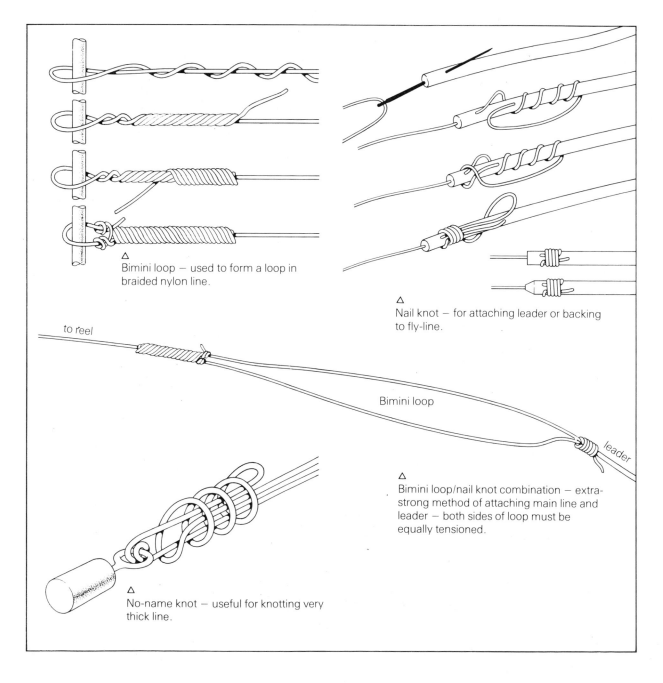

Bimini loop — used to form a loop in braided nylon line.

Nail knot — for attaching leader or backing to fly-line.

to reel

Bimini loop

leader

Bimini loop/nail knot combination — extra-strong method of attaching main line and leader — both sides of loop must be equally tensioned.

No-name knot — useful for knotting very thick line.

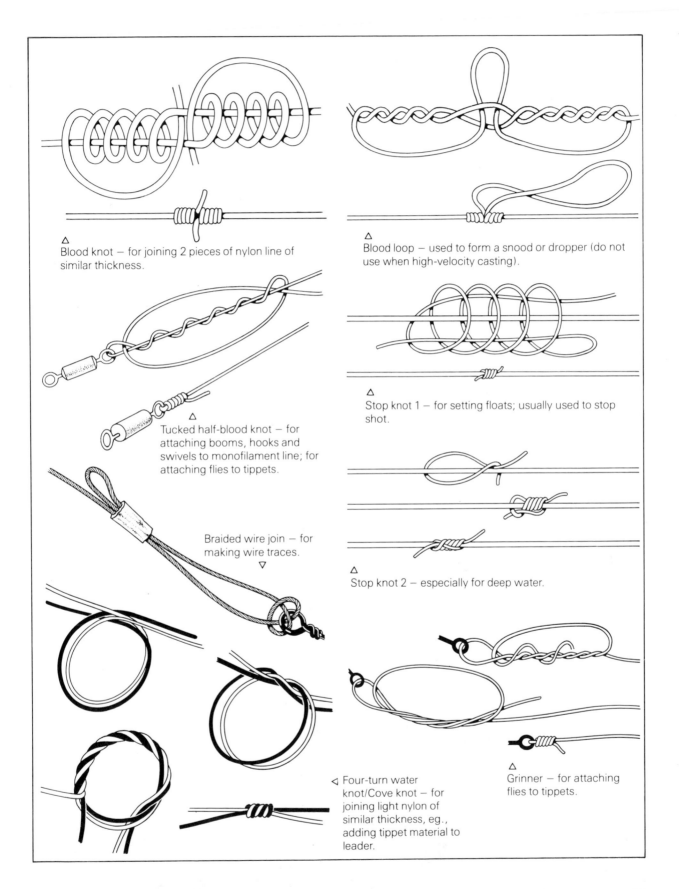

Blood knot — for joining 2 pieces of nylon line of similar thickness.

Blood loop — used to form a snood or dropper (do not use when high-velocity casting).

Tucked half-blood knot — for attaching booms, hooks and swivels to monofilament line; for attaching flies to tippets.

Stop knot 1 — for setting floats; usually used to stop shot.

Braided wire join — for making wire traces.

Stop knot 2 — especially for deep water.

◁ Four-turn water knot/Cove knot — for joining light nylon of similar thickness, eg., adding tippet material to leader.

Grinner — for attaching flies to tippets.

139

Index